Trust Is My New Skill: Building a Skilled Community

Stan Washington

Trust Is My New Skill: Building a Skilled Community

Printed in the United States of America

First Printing, 2026

ISBN: 978-0-9909831-8-7

Table of Contents

THIS IS A DO IT YOURSELF (DIY) RESOURCE

Dedication

This book is dedicated to those who feel alone and need some guidance, who can't afford business school, but need a solid foundation.

In loving memory of Preston and Susie Washington.

Acknowledgments

To the GOD-Centered Business team, I give my thanks. Growing up during the process of writing this book was difficult for me. Yet, a group of people surrounded me to help me help others. Also, thanks to my prayer partners who were able to ask GOD for the resilience and breakthroughs I am experiencing.

Stan Washington

Foreword

My heart goes out to micro-business owners who see themselves as too small to be concerned with. GOD hears you and has called me to serve you with lessons and experiences to encourage you to keep going because HE is guiding you to success.

Build a skilled community using the GOD-Centered Business Framework (Skills Inventory).

Successful businesses work well with customers, other businesses and possibly employees, contractors or volunteers. They also have a leader who can bring people together as a skilled community to deliver quality and results.

Seek Wisdom is the Skills Inventory section of the GOD-Centered Business Framework. How you manage your team and outsource people is vitally important to the success of your business.

This book will provide leadership tips to grow your resilience to face difficult people who do not seem to want you to succeed; even if the difficult person is sometimes you. This is a Do-It-Yourself resource.

As I stated before in *Active Forgiveness: Freedom to Be a Leader*, I will take you on my journey to leadership. **I will ask you challenging questions along the way**. I want you to be a whole leader who can traverse cultural and economic barriers, reaching people with the love that only comes from CHRIST. This book is made for skim reading so you can pick up vital elements quickly.

Introduction

With the project being behind, talking to the guy made me feel relieved that I could get the work done. Something was broken and I needed it fixed right away. I allowed the invoice to be paid for the remaining work to be done, but unfortunately, it was not completed like we discussed.

I had to let the contractor go. But the problem still existed. The work was incomplete. I was the contractor manager for the company, so I quickly put rules in place to never let this happen again. This was a corporate example that I remembered when I struck it out on my own.

Later, I became an entrepreneur.

Excited about being in business, I quickly posted on social media that I was ready to help the world! I did not expect as many predators as I received. I got a direct message (DM) from someone.

"*I can help you get in front of 10,000 people. DM me.*" - **Cold Call Direct Message 1**

Other messages followed.

"*What do you think about us working together on domestic and international transportation services? Can we have a quick call next week?*" - **Cold Call Direct Message 2**

"What? You don't even know what my business is?

"*I'm reaching out because I believe I can help you or your organization reduce operational workload, increase efficiency, and free up your time to focus on what matters most — growing your business.*" - **Cold Call Direct Message 3**

"How did you assess how inefficient my business is without knowing me or reviewing my business processes?" I said to myself.

These are real messages. Do they sound familiar to you? Business owners need help and are looking for answers, only to get preyed on by people who could care less about your success. You need discernment and a process for making decisions that lead to productivity.

Overcoming Feeling Lost and Getting Rid of Predator Tactics

Over the years, I have had business owners referred to me who have experienced similar cold calls or who have experienced poor workmanship.

I remember the bad experiences I encountered in the past, when I paid someone and the work was not done or it was incomplete and I did not know how to correct it and had to throw it all away.

I also remember feeling lost as a new entrepreneur and feeling like I had to become a predator, similar to the ones preying on me. This feeling raised a conflict in my beliefs in GOD. "LORD, am I the only one who feels this way?" "No!" GOD said to me.

predator – an organism (or a business person) that survives by hunting, killing, and consuming other prey (your business)

Do you have a mindset that someone has to lose in order for you to win? Let's address this mindset with "**Everyone has to win or we all lose.**"

Trust Is My New Skill
Building a Skilled Community

The world is full of poor leaders whose purpose is to gain power and money from everyone they meet, without delivering their promises. GOD challenges you and me to not be like the world, while remaining in the world. Standing up for your beliefs can make you feel alone in the business world, but you are never alone.

GOD has given you purpose to leverage the experiences you have had; to help those who seek HIM. Be aware that people with purpose can sometimes be laughed at. People with great purpose will be misunderstood. That does not diminish the purpose.

Noah had purpose that was greatly misunderstood. I wonder if Noah felt alone when GOD approached him to build an ark.

GOD introduced the problem.

Genesis 6: 5-8 –

5 Then the Lord saw that the wickedness of man was great in
the earth, and that every intent of the thoughts of his
heart was only evil continually. 6 And the Lord was sorry that He
had made man on the earth, and He was grieved in His heart. 7 So
the Lord said, "I will destroy man whom I have created from the
face of the earth, both man and beast, creeping thing and birds of
the air, for I am sorry that I have made them." 8 But Noah found
grace in the eyes of the Lord.

GOD introduced HIS solution to the problem.

Genesis 6:13-14 –

13 And God said to Noah, "The end of all flesh has come before
Me, for the earth is filled with violence through them; and behold, I
will destroy them with the earth. 14 Make yourself an ark of
gopherwood; make rooms in the ark, and cover it inside and
outside with pitch.

When it comes to solving problems you face with your business or job, I believe GOD wants you to build an ark. Not a literal ark, but a figurative one. In fact, I believe HE wants you to build three arks to address your problems and eventually help other people with theirs.

Working with People Who Think Different Than Me

Learning from leaders who acquired wealth in a predatory fashion turned me off. But it was difficult to find leaders who followed GOD and were business people. I turned to the Bible for examples. I believe the examples in the Bible are more than history lessons. For example, did you know there were three arks built in the Bible? Noah's Ark, the Bulrushes Ark for Moses and the Ark of the Covenant. I noticed that each ark played a significant role in saving mankind, raising up a leader and remembering GOD's power and deliverance. I believe you can experience their success too.

This book will discuss why you should work with purpose while working with people versus working alone. It will also show you ways to work with the variety of styles by building three types of arks GOD wants you to build:

Purpose Ark

Personal Ark

Persuasive Ark

If you will allow me to be your guide, I will provide observations from leaders like Noah, Jochebed and the Ark of the Covenant builders that I hope you can apply to your style to become a resilient leader of a profitable business or in your role at work. Each ark type will be used to handle situations and people in a way that brings productivity and peace.

By the time you read this book you should have better understanding to:

- Clearly define the purpose of your product or service to assign roles to team members.
- Make adjustments in your leadership style to work with a variety of people **while remaining encouraged to not give up!**
- Use discernment to clearly define roles that are essential for the growth of your skilled community and ultimately your business.

You Need This Book If . . .

- You are a small business owner or in a role who works alone or has a team of people.
- You need a set of skills or people who possess them.
- You have had difficulty getting along with customers, employees or employers.
- You need GOD's direction out of a difficult situation.

Features of This Book

Along with strategies you can use, at the end of each chapter, you'll find one or more of the following bulleted lists:

NEXT STEPS

This section provides three to five tips to implement after you've considered the advice in each chapter.

WARNINGS

In this section, you'll find a list of problems and pitfalls to avoid when executing the items you choose. Each section has specific warnings I collected from my experiences and from other experts to keep you from wasting time and money.

Turning "Purpose" into "Defined Work" Process

Last but not least is our process. Leaders like yourself need a process to clearly define the work you or your outsourced resource will accomplish to grow your business.

For Solo Leaders

"I am not alone. I will be provided for," is the mindset needed for this process.

For Team Leaders

"I can do this by myself, but I am better with you," is the mindset needed for this process.

Is this it!?

Fear Defined My Purpose

Survival became my purpose. To eat food, I needed money. To live some place, I needed money. To do things in the place I lived, I needed money. Let's see. Add one plus one, carry the two. Okay. In life's equation, the answer was "*I needed money!*"

My fear was that I would not be able to provide for my family, eat or pay bills.

First Time Leading a Team

"*Earn a good living by getting a job*" is what I was taught, so I did. I worked at a bowling alley, then a desk clerk, then a research assistant, then a janitor. Each of those positions required me to learn how to do the job and then do it. In other words, I had minimal interaction with my coworkers and I was not making decisions. I was doing my tasks; they were doing theirs.

But later in life I got into management. My first stretch of management had three people I had to be over. I was the employee and the three were paid contractors. The job required my team to manage a specific technology skillset. I had learned the technology, but the work was more than I could handle.

The contractors were supposed to help. I inherited the team of someone who left the company. When they arrived, they asked me what they were supposed to be doing. "I am not sure. Let me get back to you," was my response to them. I then went to my boss and asked, "What should I tell them to do?" She said, "You are the manager. Figure out what you will have them do."

This was not the answer I wanted or needed. After panicking, I sat down to develop a plan I learned from my years of being a business consultant. Someone had chosen the contractors by their skills, so I asked them what their skills were. They told me. The three skills were somewhat distinct, but overlapped slightly.

I developed written roles and responsibilities for each contractor so I could monitor the work. It felt strange to tell people what I expected them to do for the first time in my life.

First Time Firing Someone

Two of the three contractors agreed with my plan. The third wanted to do the work assigned to the other two. I reiterated his assignment, but got reports that he ignored what I told him and was doing what I gave the others to do.

I eventually had to fire him.

Expecting another contractor to be given to me, I went to my boss and said, "Can I bring on someone else?" She said, "No." Too much time had passed and some of the **budget** was already spent.

I wound up doing his work and mine. I started going to work early and coming home late. I had to be the manager and the employee because I feared getting fired. **Work had become my purpose in life**.

I would remember this story when I went into business.

Mindset for Corporate Versus Self-Employment

After delivering the project on time and on budget, I was praised for successfully leading my team to completion. I got a bonus and an award. After doing this a number of times, I got promoted. This did not prepare me to be an entrepreneur because the vision was set for me. All I had to do was execute someone else's vision well and I was rewarded for it. I had to unlearn this mindset when running a business.

At the next level, I had more people and more responsibility. Instead of doing the work, I had to rely on others to get the work done. I had to set the goals for the work to be done (**scope/work**), set a realistic timeline to completion (**schedule/time**) and set the amount needed to complete the work (**cost/budget**). This is known as the Magic Triangle of Project Management. This is something valuable that I took into entrepreneurism.

Work provided me with money, but I thought about the problems of work a lot. I would wake up in the middle of the night thinking of solutions to problems my team would face. Meanwhile at home, my family and I had just bought a house, cars and all the stuff the house and cars could hold. I worried about keeping all the stuff. The same worries would occur when I became an entrepreneur.

As the bills piled up, so did the need to keep a high-paying job. One time on one job, I worked twenty-four hours straight. Unfortunately, this would not be the only time. **My purpose had now become acquiring and holding onto stuff**.

Purpose Conflict

After delivering yet another project successfully, I needed a vacation. I had worked with a group of employees and outside contractors to build cutting edge training systems the company had never seen. I performed so well, that my boss and my boss's boss would be invited to go on lavish vacation. Apparently, the work that I was doing was getting notice inside the company. It wasn't just the work, but how I brought teams together to work without quarrels.

My boss's boss approached me on the vacation. He was going to be named a CEO of a company and wanted me to be the Chief Information Officer (CIO). You couldn't believe my excitement! There is no way I would become an entrepreneur.

I went to the interview nervous. They asked me one question that took me out of the running. "Would you be able to get rid of thirty-three percent of the staff?" "No!" was my answer. I was taken out of consideration. I licked my wounds and pondered if I was cut out to be a "leader." I was, but a different leader than they expected.

When I got back to my job, it seemed bland now. The excitement I once put into the position now seemed mundane, with nowhere to go from here. After some time, my boss came to me and said, "You still have to do this job." This was a wake-up call to me that my performance was slipping.

To make matters worse, a reorganization happened and I would no longer report to the team that made me rise to internal stardom. I had to get used to a new boss and a new role with new pressure. My purpose in life was to make money, but the people I had to deal with were not great. **My purpose of working and paying bills seemed to be getting me tired**.

Purpose Ark

I went to church and the pastor asked me to go on a mission trip with him. I describe this experience in *Active Forgiveness: Freedom to Be a Leader*. I remember the contentment I experienced when I was there. It was a mountaintop experience that would only be felt once in my lifetime.

When I got home, the warm sensation of service that filled my heart, quickly disappeared. I was back to the grind where people were not content, but contemptuous. One day I thought to myself, "***Is this it? Is this my entire purpose in life?***" Have you ever felt like this or asked this question? If so, then perhaps GOD wants you to build an ark.

A life without purpose can be wasted. I believe GOD wants to give you purpose greater than paying bills, so HE wants you to build a **Purpose Ark** to clearly explain what your business offers and what GOD offers. Aligning to GOD helps your business have a greater purpose to keep you going when times get difficult. In the book of Genesis, Noah was told by GOD to build an ark for HIS purpose of saving mankind.

GOD had seen how evil HIS creation had become and was willing to wipe it out. HE created humans with free will to choose HIM but they were choosing their own way. In fact, they were choosing to be against HIM as the creator.

He told Noah about HIS plan to flood the earth. This gave Noah purpose. Noah tried to save his siblings, friends and neighbors to no avail. But I believe he tried.

purpose - a person's sense of resolve or determination – design or intend (something) for a particular use – have (something) as one's intention or objective.

"all this God purposed, and all this he has accomplished"

Personal Ark

When I returned from mission trip, I saw life differently. I attended a men's conference and heard a speaker give us a challenge. "Huddle up in groups of four and discuss this question, 'If you knew your life would end in two weeks, how would you live it differently?'"

Some said they would tell people "I love you" more often and others said they would apologize to people. I agreed. But GOD was tugging at my heart and my answer was that I would tell people to believe in JESUS with all their heart. Eternal life with GOD felt so valuable to me.

The speaker then said, “Then why not live your life like that every day?” This challenge was impactful to me, which brings me to the next ark I believe GOD wants you to build, namely the **Personal Ark** to prepare yourself for life’s difficulties while remaining in business and aligning to GOD.

During the birth of Moses, Pharaoh was a harsh, erratic and insecure leader of his nation. He put wild rules in place like “Any male born must be thrown into the river.” Moses’s mother could not follow this rule, nor could any Hebrew woman.

They feared GOD and protected the babies. Moses’s mother made an ark to save him. This ark only had room for one. Moses would be saved by this ark and would become a great leader of many people. I believe GOD wants you to build a **Personal Ark** that broadens your leadership style and keeps your mood at higher levels.

personal development - a lifelong process of improving oneself through conscious actions, learning, and self-reflection to reach one’s full potential

Persuasive Ark

There are times when we feel like everything is going wrong. Problems in life or with the business can seem to come faster than you can handle. You finally break down and get some help, only to be burned by poor quality, unfinished work and completely wrong items. This can be very frustrating and cause some people to become tyrants. GOD sees tyrants and hears the cries of HIS people who are oppressed. HE hears your cries and wants you to be a leader who is persuasive to get quality work done while raising up disciples for HIM. HE wants you to build a **Persuasive Ark** to get the work done while building disciples who can have hope and face life's difficulties.

GOD will deliver you. Here is a quick summary of the deliverance of GOD's people from oppression to being placed into the Promised Land that I will use as examples of how GOD works with HIS leaders.

After the Pharaoh who did not know Joseph died, another tyrant was put in his place. **The people groaned because the work was so hard**. GOD heard their cry and said HE would deliver them.

GOD performed ten plagues on Egypt, causing them to let GOD's people leave. During this time Aaron's staff became a serpent as a sign of GOD's power. It turned back into a staff.

Plague 1 – Water Becomes Blood

Plague 2 – Frogs

Plague 3 – Lice

Plague 4 – Flies

Plague 5 – Diseased Livestock

Plague 6 – Boils

Plague 7 – Hail

Plague 8 – Locusts

Plague 9 – Darkness

Plague 10 – Death of the Firstborn

Pharaoh finally let the people go. **One month into the exit, the people complained**, saying the trip was too hard and they should have stayed in Egypt as slaves because they had food to eat.

GOD provided quail and manna to eat every day.

GOD told Moses to preserve some manna in a jar.

GOD provided the Ten Commandments.

GOD told Moses to make an ark.

Aaron's staff budded, blossomed and produced ripe almonds!

This staff was preserved in the Ark of the Covenant along with the jar of manna, along with the Ten Commandments that were written in stone by the hand of GOD. I believe the elements of this ark were used to persuade people to keep their faith in the power that GOD had shown. I also believe that GOD wants you to build a **Persuasive Ark** to build a skilled community that you influence, for the growth of your business and to guide people to HIM through the growth you experience.

persuade – cause (someone) to do something through reasoning or argument – cause (someone) to believe something, especially after a sustained effort; convince

All three arks that GOD wants you to build will give you purpose, grow you personally and help you persuade people. "Why?" you may ask. Because GOD wants to include you in HIS wonderful plan HE has for those who love HIM. HE wants you! HE is concerned about your concerns and wants you to be aligned with HIM.

Who am I?

Know Yourself and Love Yourself

Trying to fit in was like watching a comedy when it came to my life. A good friend told me about little league tryouts and I figured I would go for it since he was interested. My brother was athletic, and I could not seem to catch anything, nor did I have interest in doing so. This would possibly by my chance to fit in with his crowd as well. When I got to the tryout, I was asked if I had a baseball glove. "Yes," I replied. Before I left the house, I found one of my brother's gloves. I didn't know how to use it.

The coach said, "Great! Go out to center field and I will hit a few balls to you. "Where is center field?" was my question. He politely pointed me to where I should stand. He hit several balls towards me. I caught zero. In fact, I closed my eyes and ran from them, not wanting to get hurt.

My batting attempts were just as comical. I threw the bat by accident as I swung wildly. Tryouts back then were to determine who would be on the "A" team or the "B" team or on the team at all. His question was relieving to me. "Are you sure you want to do this?" I smiled and said, "No!" I was glad I could be me! He said, "Maybe next year." I became a bowler instead.

Leadership Tip #1 – Your business or job needs you to be the best version of yourself without comparison to other people.

Love Yourself in a Balanced Way

I was choosing my own crowd. Fortunately for me, the experiences I had with bullies kept me from hanging around people who wanted to harm others. I didn't want to be a thug, but I wanted to fit in somewhere. One family asked me to go bowling with them. I loved it. Another person asked me if I wanted to go camping with the scouts, another asked if I wanted to learn about computers. My sister and my friends had me playing games. My parents taught me about CHRIST. My interests were being shaped and I was thankful for each experience. I started liking who I was. Do you like who you are? This is important.

When I was younger, I looked at my deficiencies and saw that I was skinny, had nappy hair, broke, and had mismatched tattered clothes. But the more I grew up, the more I realized that **trying to please people** by changing who I was would never get me anywhere. I tried! My insecurities took me down the path of blaming people, labeling people and comparing myself with other people.

In college I had to write a speech about my life. I told people that I was teased for being too skinny. That was something I could not change. I had to start liking who I was before I could like anyone else.

I Started Liking Me

When I started liking who I was, I saw GOD differently. At one point I saw HIM as a being I should blame for my life being a mess. But in reality, my life was much better than I thought. **I had to stop comparing myself to everyone else to see that I am loved by GOD, period**!

In my speech I said. "You may think I am too skinny, but my question to you is, 'Too skinny for what?'" I enjoyed saying that. Overconfidence was not my problem. I had low self-esteem that made me think people could not like me for me.

But who am I? I am a smiler. I enjoy laughter, but not at someone else's expense. I am a thinker and I am very tenacious. Believe it or not, I am quite shy, but can be gregarious when needed. I love being alone, and I love being around people. I get energized by sitting quietly and I get energized being in a crowd. I am serious and goofy. Trying to label me is difficult to impossible. I am a writer but not a reader. But I am a visual learner who can read instructions. Go figure.

GOD Made Me

One day I stumbled on a verse that helped me like who I was. Psalm 139:14 –

I will praise You, for I am fearfully and wonderfully made;
Marvelous are Your works,
And that my soul knows very well.

When I read this passage of scripture, I see GOD taking time to make me versus speaking me into existence. HE fashioned Adam out of the dirt and breathed life into him and he became a living soul. HE spoke everything else into existence, but took HIS time with humans.

HE did the same for Eve. HE created her different, yet equal to Adam. Harmony was created. HE did the same with you and me. HE took HIS time creating every hair on your head. HE loves the hairy and the hairless. I say that because you should see my bald head now.

I truly believe that if you don't love how GOD made you, you will have trouble thinking humans can love you. You will put them through unnecessary tests, mislabel them and compare yourself to them.

The Psalmist only focuses on how GOD made him. He then turns to the fact that GOD has HIS own works that you and I can be part of. "*Marvelous are YOUR works*" seems to be an acknowledgement that GOD is doing some incredible stuff that HE wants you a part of.

How you see yourself affects your business or job. If you feel inadequate, then the wolves who prey on sheep will devour your profits. Your desire for affirmation could cause you to spend unnecessary money seeking "likes" versus actual sales. Your business may need revision, but you may feel too insecure to get feedback. You may also have been tricked into becoming too prideful to believe anything is wrong. I am not talking about arrogant pride, rather **scared pride**, when life has beat up on you so much that you fall into a self-protective trap that everyone else is wrong.

How well do you know you?

Take a moment and look at this picture from the *GOD-Centered Business: A Framework to Grow with Resilience* book to identify how you operate.

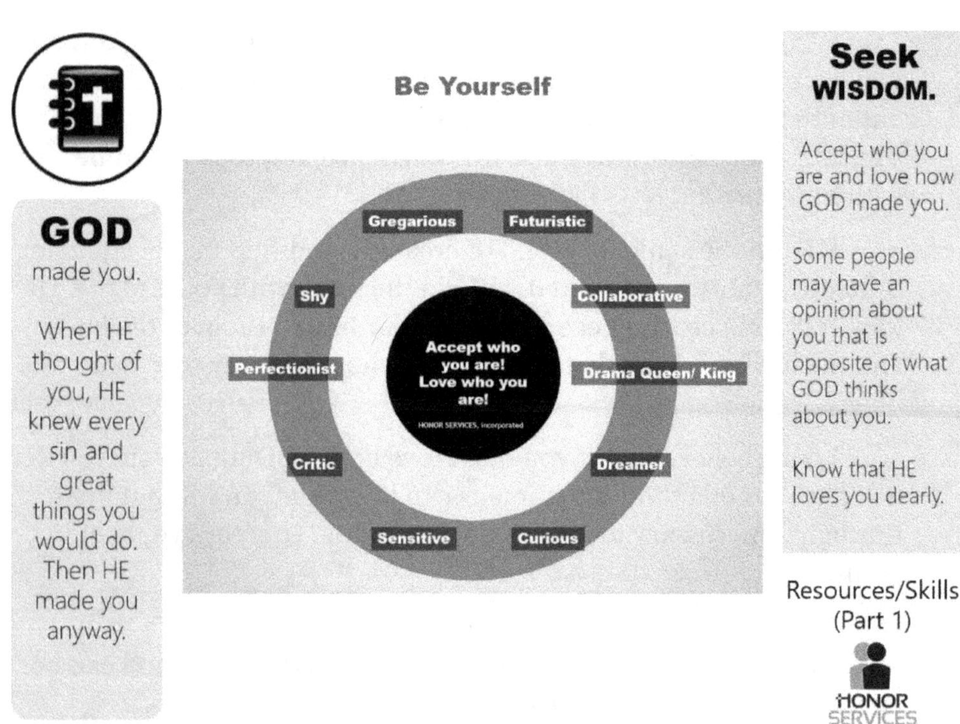

Working alone can be a result of not having enough finances to pay for a team, but sometimes it could stem from not liking yourself. While this seems extreme, it needs to be considered. Your approach to customers and business partners can be affected by **insecurities** or **overconfidence** if you have either. Both extremes can cause issues with how you work with employees, contractors or volunteers. It can also affect your purpose.

How did GOD make you? What parts of you need to be tamed and what parts of you need to be unchained from the bondage of society? Are you overlooking the gifts and talents GOD has given you? How does your thinking affect your trust in GOD? I will go more into detail about this when you are building your **Personal Ark**.

Let's look at working with trust.

I am doing everything by myself!

Who Do I Trust?

When I graduated from the University of Illinois, Champaign-Urbana, I needed to be trained. There were no YouTube videos or quick ways to pick up the skills needed in programming at that time. My boss gave me an assignment that I had no idea what he was talking about. I frustrated him by asking him questions every ten minutes. Finally, I said to myself, "You better learn this or you are out." My boss gave me a programming book and I stayed at work late at night learning how to create applications the way the company needed me to do.

I got good at software engineering. In fact, I got so good, that people were asking me questions. My confidence was sky-high. My ability to learn new things did not come from having help or guidance, but out being alone and still needing to perform. I was failing miserably and needed to learn. Once I learned, I began to trust myself, maybe a little too much.

Today's Giants Are Mean and Scary

Today's giants are different. There are more demands and more challenges to overcome. The expectation that "*you should know this*" is an arrogant spirit that prevails throughout society. Meanwhile, you have to learn how to run a business or do your job

Leadership Tip #2 – Consider bartering services if you are not funded. GOD will provide!

using the latest and greatest tactics. It can be overwhelming. It can also introduce fear which attacks your trust which introduces a limiting belief of needing to be great at everything by yourself.

Many business owners work alone for a variety of reasons. These self-employed business owners, do it all. They think of the business idea, make the solution, market it, sell it and do it all again the next day. Are you a business owner who works alone or do you work alone on a job?

Fear-Based Decisions

When I first got into business, I was scared half to death. Jobs could not be found anywhere, or at least I couldn't' find one. Bills were piling up and I felt I needed to bring in some income. Someone said to me, "What do you like to do?" This question was to calm me down enough to think about what business I should go into.

I said that I liked to help people with their careers. "There you go," she said vaguely. I started researching and ran into resources at the Small Business Administration. I read all the information and attended classes. I coupled this information with the information I learned while working for large corporations.

I was working out of fear versus fact. I felt I needed to make money fast, so I listened to rumors of what people were doing to become successful. I was easy prey for those who wanted my money, but fortunately in my previous corporate role, I could see through hustlers. I enlisted people who made me successful in a corporation I worked for.

What Is My Vision?

There are many people out there who are willing to take you off of the **destination** you have set for your company. They will try to convince you to use their product or service without knowing your **destination**, causing you to detour from your **destination**. Soon you will find yourself without results and even worse, have to backtrack from their detour. Meanwhile, you still have to reach your **destination** and are stuck at the point of the detour.

Proverbs 29:18a –

Where there is no vision, the people perish (KJV)

I was used to setting the vision for corporate employees, but I could not quite explain what a small business vision was to my business clients. Years later I came up with this definition of the vision:

A vision is simply a destination you want to go to, and the steps you will take to get there. I will use the term "destination" often referring to this definition. Without a destination, you will not know where you are going. You set the destination for each person who works on building your Business Features. **A Business Feature is an item your business does or sells.**

GOD Sent Help

I did not feel I had the skills that it would take to run the business I chose. I started a professional resume writing business, since "everyone" was out of work, or at least many people I knew were unemployed. **I started a business that was safe because I was cautious and needed to learn before I jumped into larger endeavors**. I also wanted to do something different than tech. I was trying to be something different than my giftedness.

GOD sent me a professional resume writer who was remarkable. I became a career coach and would pay her for her services. I had to pay for the artwork of a logo and I needed a website, so I hired a web developer. I got a contract with the federal government to help guide those who were transitioning from the Air Force to the work force.

The business was simple but made very little profit. Years into it, as I went to sleep one night, GOD finally spoke to me. I mean, what took HIM so long? HE told me to be grateful for the skills and experiences HE has taken me through over the years.

Inventory of My Skills

After hearing this in my spirit, **I did an inventory of my skills that I was thankful for**. These are my differentiators.

1. I led people to clarity well.
2. I put people at ease.
3. I had a broad understanding of technology.
4. I knew what business operations was.
5. I managed large budgets and knew why.
6. I understood influence, awareness, self-control and other soft-skills.
7. I loved GOD

I felt that GOD was telling me to return to my giftedness HE exposed me to, namely my technology roots that I abandoned when coaching. I commissioned developers, graphic designers and marketing people.

This time I had a vision and I knew what each person needed to do. And I had a new skill added to me by being able to guide businesses in explaining who they are. I learned this skill from the resume business. What skills do you have? What has GOD exposed you to that would benefit HIS people?

Working with Human Assumptions

I knew exactly what I needed the developers to build. I knew exactly what the marketing people needed to say and I knew what the graphics design person needed to produce. This time the business was successful, to a point. I built a Contact Relationship Management (CRM) tool. Business started taking off! Unfortunately, some people would sign up to use my CRM, but would go out of business in three to six months. Not everyone, but enough. **I assumed the problem was marketing**. What assumptions are you making?

I tried to stop the bleeding by writing a marketing book, *Plans to Prosper: Strategies, Systems & Tools for Small Business Marketing Success*. My business grew, but some people were still going out of business. I felt I needed to come up with a solution.

GOD Challenged Me

GOD challenged me one day. HE kept asking me over and over, "Who's business is this?" HE kept me awake for hours. I finally gave in and said to HIM, "YOURS. The business is YOURS." HE told me to feed HIS sheep. HE then said something strange, "Get rid of your current customers and start over with MY foundation."

No business person alive would do this! I wanted to be obedient, so I sent emails letting each customer know that I needed to start over, this time with GOD at the center of my business. Many returned, but not all. I felt nervous letting customers go but this time I had to put my **trust in GOD** versus on my own abilities. Who are you placing your trust in? Do you only trust yourself? Are you trusting the latest rumor or the fastest technology answer? What gifts are you overlooking that GOD wants you to use? Are you operating in fear?

Trust Is My New Skill

GOD wants you to have abundant life. But sometimes the abundance can look different than you expect. HE may give you an abundance of people to pray for or serve. HE may give you an abundance of wealth for the sole purpose of being generous. HE may even give you an abundance of problems that only HE can solve so your praises can be heard globally as you tell others how GOD delivered you.

I finally had to trust GOD with my business versus trying to get HIM to do my bidding or to manipulate HIM. I haven't looked back since! GOD was my missing foundation. Are you ready to begin trusting GOD?

Here is a verse my mom would repeat almost every time we would speak.

Proverbs 3:5 – 6 –

5 Trust in the Lord with all your heart,
And lean not on your own understanding;
6 In all your ways acknowledge Him,
And He shall direct your paths.

There were times when I placed my full trust in GOD, but there were also times when I placed my full trust in my abilities, and I would become exhausted. One day, I had more problems than abilities. It seemed like relationships were breaking, business was failing, finances were disappearing and people around me were ailing. GOD said to me, "Will you trust ME?"

I pondered the scripture for a long time. "Am I leaning to my own understanding?" I asked myself. I listened to a sermon that mentioned the verse above. With everything falling apart I said, "Yes, I will trust YOU."

Trust Is My New Skill
Building a Skilled Community

Trust became my new skill and because of that, GOD gave me purpose. Let's take a look at telling your employees, contractors or volunteers about the purpose of your business.

Do I have Buy-In?

Build a Purpose Ark to Provide Clarity

Not knowing where to start, I was told to think of a name for my business, then come up with a logo, then start working on a website. I was also told that I needed help with marketing, sales, leads, and groups that would help me meet celebrities. Does this sound familiar to you? They cold called me with pitches to save my company without knowing what my company did or sold.

Remembering some of the poor leaders I worked for; I decided to be different so I wrote out what my company provided and why. I did not want to be like the uncaring leaders I encountered, so I had to develop my own culture for my company. I also had to get the work done. I brought on people to help me build my Business

> Leadership Tip #3 – Have a purpose for everything you do. Be GOD's purpose maker.

Features. I looked back on my first time I led a team and remembered how nervous I was to be setting the steps for all the workers. This time I knew what to do, but I did not know if it would work. I had never been in business for myself on this scale.

I started doing a lot of BUSY activities. I went to a lot of classes, getting taught things I already knew but was unsure of myself. It "felt" good to be busy, but I needed to be productive. What is the difference? I was guessing at the things I needed to do. I spent a lot of time alone and I asked GOD to **bless my guess.** When my guess did not work, I would have to start over on another guess. We call this a pivot. **Being productive is working on the right things that will make my company profitable while providing a great product or service**. My company brought in money, but was not profitable. I needed help. I guessed at the resume and career business because of my fear of losing money.

It was an easy business to start, but I did not understand the emotional block people faced when losing a job or trying to change careers. I also did not understand the massive number of hours it would take to coach someone to success because their life may have been the thing holding them back from making good vital decisions.

I also did not understand the nature of serving a business versus serving the consumer directly. I thought I could grow a business where the customer paid for my product or service. I did not realize that I needed to have business processes in place that would help me scale or grow my business versus simply "doing" the business.

I went back to my corporate roots and looked at the business processes that made them grow into large corporations. Many of the businesses I worked for served businesses that served consumers. The corporations also helped their businesses become profitable through the use of their product or service. Are you helping other businesses become successful or are you helping the customer? This needs to be decided. I recommend you do one or the other first, but not tackle both at the same time. Your purpose message will become mixed. Let's talk a little about purpose.

Purpose

What is the purpose of your business? Wrestle with this statement for a minute because you may have written some words on a vision board or business plan that does not truly answer the question. What product do you make and why? What service do you provide and why? Are you solving the problems of the business you are serving? What group needs this, wants this and have actually asked for this? Should you sell to businesses who will in turn sell to their customers? Or, should you sell directly to customers which may feel comfortable, but may not bring in as many sales? If this product or service is a new concept, then how will it save time, money or effort? How is GOD using you to reach HIS Kingdom?

It takes trust to be guided where GOD wants you to go. Business to Business (B2B) and Business to Consumer (B2C) are the two routes of providing your product or service. Let me give you an example of how things are changing in those spaces. Restaurants used to provide B2C service only. A customer would walk in, order food, eat it, pay and leave. But today, many restaurants provide catering services for business lunches and banquet dinners. They are both B2B and B2C. They are solving the problem of keeping business discussion going over lunch. Which are you? How is GOD stretching you?

Before you went into business you should have answered these questions. You may have done this and may fully understand the purpose of your business. But now you need some help. You realize your skills are limited and you need other people to achieve the company's purpose of being profitable.

You may run into a situation where the work has stopped because you do not have the skill to do a particular thing. You know the work to do, but do not know how to do it. You may even know how to do something, but do not have the right resources to do it. You need a **skill** and **buy-in** to keep your business going. You may need a **Purpose Ark.**

"What is an ark?" you may ask.

ark

1. (in the Bible) the ship built by Noah to save his family and two of every kind of animal from the Flood; Noah's ark

2. short for Ark of the Covenant

3. (in the Bible) the small vessel built by Jochebed, Moses's Mother, that protected Moses as a baby

I am not asking you to become a boat builder. The **Purpose Ark** is a figurative platform of purpose for you and your business.

The ark I will focus on right now is the one that was built to save Noah and his family. The example is misleading. The real purpose for saving Noah, his family, insects and animals was to continue life.

What does this have to do with your business? You may desire to continue the life of your business. You must bring your family, friends, workers, volunteers along on the journey of fulfilling the purpose to your customer.

Purpose Ark

Building a Purpose Ark is a process to document an individualized, revision oriented, role definition that guides the employee, contractor, volunteer, family member or friend to buy-in to achieving the company's mission, goals and values that GOD has called you to do, while addressing current issues and preventing a breakdown in acceptance.

Whether you work alone or with one other person or a team, you will need buy-in to achieve true success. **Buy-in is belief, acceptance and understanding to the point of profitable action**. Without buy-in, you may fall into a trap of seeking affirmation which could be very expensive. Some people pay for social media "likes" and get no sales because they want affirmation versus buy-in.

The purpose of your product or service needs to be obvious to the buyer. If you are a business who sells to other businesses, have you researched what their business sells or does? Let's look at our example of selling cakes. If you sell to a vending machine business, then have you considered, delivery, packaging sizes, freshness date visibility, and access to the machine? What if the vending machine was located in a restricted area? Do you have access? Your buy-in needs to include answers.

It takes time to achieve buy-in from various people in your circle of influence. People who say they are fully behind you may not understand the entirety of the vision GOD has for you in this business. This is not their fault. GOD spoke to you about the vision for the business. Their lack of understanding needs you to help them understand the purpose GOD has in your life and the purpose you need them to fill. See what GOD said to Noah.

GOD introduced HIS solution to the problem in

Genesis 6:13-14 –

13 *And God said to Noah, "The end of all flesh has come before Me, for the earth is filled with violence through them; and behold, I will destroy them with the earth.* 14 *Make yourself an ark of gopherwood; make rooms in the ark, and cover it inside and outside with pitch.*

Observation 1: GOD speaks to you, not everyone around you.

What I noticed is GOD spoke to Noah only. HE did not speak to his family. Noah had to tell his family what was going on and keep them informed on when GOD would execute HIS plan.

Your business should not be a place of pain, rather a place of peace. When GOD speaks to you, understand that the people around you may not know what is really going on.

Imagine Noah having to tell his family that it is going to rain when it had never, ever rained in all of history. Also imagine Noah trying to convince his siblings that a flood was coming when it had never flooded. Noah had to get buy-in from his family to sustain all of life. Was this a little pressure? The scripture never shows Noah pressuring his family, but I believe he worked with urgency.

Noah had a purpose that could not be derailed by other people. He focused his attention on his purpose and could not be deterred.

What is GOD saying for you to do or become? What is the purpose for each worker? What purpose has GOD given you?

Write the purpose for each person working for you in your ***Purpose Ark***.

Take a look at the following example illustrations:

Purpose Ark Example 1 – Obtain purpose for your Business Feature from GOD.

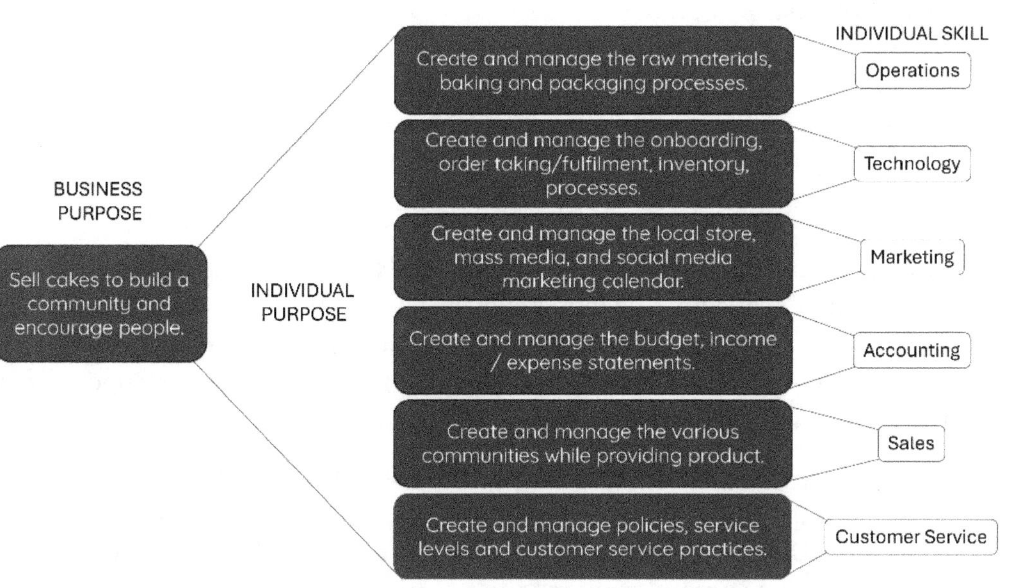

Purpose Ark Example 2 – Translate the business purpose into individualized role definitions.

Observation 2: GOD gives clear instructions.

Speaking of work, GOD gave Noah explicit instructions on how to build the ark. The thing I notice is GOD gave clear instructions. When you bring on employees, contractors or volunteers, you should have clear, explicit instructions for them to do their work. If you do not have clear instructions, do not bring on the worker. Imagine hiring a home renovation contractor and the day they arrive, they ask you, "What would you like us to renovate?" If your reply is, "I don't know; what skills do you have and how can you help me?" they will leave quickly.

Know the purpose for each worker, including yourself. Yes, you have a purpose. As the business owner, you should be bringing work, resources and best practices to your business to fulfill its purpose.

Write clear instructions for each worker including yourself in your ***Purpose Ark****.*

Observation 3: GOD has a bigger plan that includes you.

The last thing I notice is GOD was saving Noah, to save humans, to produce JESUS as a human, so HE could be killed, and resurrected to save anyone who believes. GOD's purpose was to save Noah to save humanity, and HIS purpose should also be recognized by you. Once I realized that I am HIS creation, I could acknowledge that HE is welcome to do whatever HE pleases with my life.

When I am open to HIS leading, HE will do amazing things in my life. Unfortunately, many people try to use GOD instead of being used by GOD. In my life, I noticed GOD shrinking back when I try to use HIM versus surrendering my life to be used by HIM. Fortunately for me, HE is the ultimate forgiver. HE gently corrects me to help me realize that HE is GOD and I am HIS creation. My purpose is HIS purpose.

Trust Is My New Skill
Building a Skilled Community

Think of a time when you had a particular skill and were asked to use it. When you received a clear request for the use of your skill, were you able to fulfill the request? I would be able to. Be clear with your purpose and those you commission to do the work. It will all come together. How will you maximize the use of skilled people?

If you do not know what the people should be doing, then that is where the business is broken. Ask GOD for clarity on the vision for the business. Again, what is the purpose of your product or service? Start there and relook at the customer's needs to see if you are missing what to deliver or how you should deliver it.

GOD is so gentle and powerful at the same time. HE cares enough for you and me to have a personal relationship with HIM. That's the next ark.

Write GOD's purpose for you in your ***Purpose Ark.***

WARNING

- Making your "child" the purpose of your business requires specific nurturing that fosters excitement in the business.
- Do not treat "adding purpose" as an exercise, rather a way of life.
- Remember to include yourself and your relationship with GOD as your purpose.

NEXT STEPS

- When defining purpose for each role, consider the finished product or service you want them to complete.
- Consider what you will have the person do within a specific span of time.
- Do not leave this chapter without practicing. Document one role before moving on. This way the examples in the next section will deepen your understanding.

You are more special than you think.

Build a Personal Ark to Become Unshakeable

I never thought of myself as special. It seemed like I had to work hard just to get to average. But GOD kept putting me in situations that would stretch my belief in HIM and myself. I did not like the small town I went to for my first job out of college, but I found myself unable to find a job to get out. I was alone and couldn't leave. The quiet seemed so loud, I couldn't stand it!

But after a while, I got used to it. I began to quiet down to listen to GOD. And better yet, hear from HIM through HIS word by reading the Bible. I said to GOD, "If YOU want me to stay here, then I will." I began to serve teens at church. After some months, a recruiter called me with a job in my home town. Now I didn't want to leave because I cared for my Sunday School class participants.

> Leadership Tip #4 – Surrender whatever percentage of your life that you want GOD to bless. HE seems to work on invitation only.

Working with People Who Think Different Than Me

Surrender takes courage. It is different than giving up on life, rather it is a very strategic move for GOD's leaders. Saying, "LORD, YOU can steer my life the way YOU want to," is the best strategic move you can make. While you care deeply about yourself, GOD will grow you to care deeply about other people.

After surrendering to GOD, life becomes more than getting your way. You start wanting more for other people and less for yourself. You actually start **caring** like JESUS.

The next ark I will focus on is the ark Jochebed built, namely the Bulrushes Ark. This is a lesser-known ark, but extremely necessary and powerful. Your **Purpose Ark** will be fulfilled by completing your **Personal Ark**.

Building a Personal Ark is a process to document a statement of values from which <u>you</u> will operate; that expresses caring, protection and recognition of something special in everyone you meet, including some enemies, for the purpose of getting profitable work done while helping them self-discover JESUS as their daily leader and Savior.

Let's test this definition with the people you have met in the past. When someone popped up and said they would "save" your business through the use of their business, did you care for that person? Were you willing to protect the person when they made a mistake or multiple mistakes? Did you see what GOD saw in the person? My honest statement to those questions was **no**. First, I just met the person and I don't know their true capabilities. And second, I only cared about what the person could do for me so I could make money!

Desiring to use people without caring for them may be the reason for a high turnover experienced by many business owners.

You Have to Know You Are Cared For

Caring for other people was not new to me, but there were periods of times when I cared for others more than I cared about myself. When things were going well, I could easily pray for people, give large amounts and cry with people. But when it came to myself; I was not generous or gracious. **I was hard on myself**. Sometimes I wondered if people cared about me or if GOD cared. **I was feeling insecure**. When times were difficult and I felt I had no one to talk to, **I felt alone. I was in a dangerous place where the enemy wanted me to doubt GOD's love**. Where do you run to when you feel that people do not care for you or about you?

Caring for people begins with you asking GOD if HE cares for you. I think you should have a great conversation with GOD, wrestling with your beliefs in the Bible. Let HIM show you how much HE cares and allow HIM to open your eyes to how much HE has cared for you all your life. If you feel that GOD doesn't care for you, then how will you be able to show anyone you care?

GOD Cares Verses

Need proof that GOD cares for you and others? Check out how much HE cares as HE inspired a variety of writers:

1 Peter 5:6-7 –

[6] Therefore humble yourselves under the mighty hand of God, that He may exalt you in due time, [7] casting all your care upon Him, for He cares for you.

Matthew 10:29-31 –

[29] Are not two sparrows sold for a copper coin? And not one of them falls to the ground apart from your Father's will. [30] But the

very hairs of your head are all numbered. [31] Do not fear therefore; you are of more value than many sparrows.

Isaiah 41:10 –

[10] Fear not, for I am with you;
Be not dismayed, for I am your God.
I will strengthen you,
Yes, I will help you,
I will uphold you with My righteous right hand.'

And lastly,

John 3:16 – 17 –

[16] For God so loved the world that He gave His only begotten Son, that whoever believes in Him should not perish but have everlasting life. [17] For God did not send His Son into the world to condemn the world, but that the world through Him might be saved.

You can rest assured that GOD cares for you and loves you deeply. **Insecurity, doubt and loneliness can blind you to GOD's care for you and others**. It will cause you to either micromanage people or heap unhealthy expectations on them within their pay grade. You have to know, that you know, that you know, that you KNOW, that GOD loves and cares for you!

This is the first part of your **Personal Ark**. *Write down how much GOD cares for you.* How will you help others self-discover how much GOD loves them? **Will you be able to slow down to get to know people before commissioning them to do the work?** Will you care about more than their results?

GOD Protects Verses

Next you have to know HE **protects** you.

2 Thessalonians 3:3 –

3 *But the Lord is faithful, and he will strengthen you and protect you from the evil one.* (NIV)

Psalm 121:7-8 –

7 *The Lord will keep you from all harm—*
he will watch over your life;
8 *the Lord will watch over your coming and going*
both now and forevermore. (NIV)

Proverbs 18:10 –

10 *The name of the Lord is a strong tower;*
The righteous run to it and are safe.

Psalm 91:1-4 –

He who dwells in the secret place of the Most High
Shall abide under the shadow of the Almighty.
2 *I will say of the Lord, "He is my refuge and my fortress;*
My God, in Him I will trust."

3 *Surely He shall deliver you from the snare of the fowler*
And from the perilous pestilence.
4 *He shall cover you with His feathers,*
And under His wings you shall take refuge;
His truth shall be your shield and buckler.

GOD Is Protecting Your Peace

I think people want the verses I just quoted to mean there will be no troubles in life. JESUS wants you to have resilience by telling us the truth.

John 16:33 –

These things I have spoken to you, that in Me you may have peace. In the world you will have tribulation; but be of good cheer, I have overcome the world."

I believe that if you place your full trust in the world, you will have tribulation or troubles with no place to escape them. But if you put your full trust in the LORD, you will have peace in the middle of the tribulations the world throws at you. JESUS has overcome the world despite the situations we face. **GOD protects our peace** even when the wheels are falling off of our lives.

After being bullied, robbed, fired, slandered and attacked, you would think that GOD is missing from my life. But I am here to tell you that I am still here and HE does care! You are now becoming a resilient leader.

How will you protect those who you have commissioned to do the work? How will you have them carve out time to get the work done with quality? How will you protect their information and your information so you both can work together without suspicion? Can you slow down to validate whether this person is truly capable of completing the work? Have you asked for a capabilities statement? When will you pray for those who work with you?

Write down your protection statement based on these questions and more that you can think of in your ***Personal Ark****.*

People Are Special to GOD

The last part of the **Personal Ark** is to recognize that every human GOD created is special and dear to HIM, even those who currently may be doing evil. I say *currently* because a famous author, Paul, persecuted the church when his name was Saul. GOD reached him and he changed. Anyone can change.

GOD also spoke through HIS servant John.

John 13:34 – 35 –

*34 A new commandment I give to you, that you love one
another; as I have loved you, that you also love one another. 35 By
this all will know that you are My disciples, if you have love for one
another."*

In this new command that JESUS gave to us, HE is not selective. "Love one another" is not exclusive or conditional. Double-minded people easily create enemies. They hate people they have not met or personally encountered.

Do you dislike or even hate certain world leaders who are hurting people? Understandable. But GOD has them. HE will pour out HIS vengeance on them. Our job is to focus on what GOD says, "Love one another." When we do this, we let go of what we think GOD should be doing.

Are you using skilled people to build your Business Features? I have heard business owners answer this question with assurance without considering they may be underestimating the capabilities needed. Let's look at the business owner who asks, "Are you good with technology?" to their cousin Bud versus doing research into what the skill actually requires.

Cousin Bud says, "I can do it." Here are his capabilities:	Skill Really Needed:
Website Page Development	Website Page Development
	Access Security
	Database queries / security
	Payment Card Industry Compliance
	Data Transport Security
	eCommerce workflow knowledge
	Broad range of industries
	Email security and workflow

In the example above, many business owners fall in the trap of getting "it" done, while leaving themselves and their customers vulnerable to attacks. "It" needs more definition and clarity.

Use Active Forgiveness

GOD wants us to actively forgive people who were supposed to perform a skill, but did not. Learn how to forgive your enemies and yourself in *Active Forgiveness: Freedom to Be a Leader*. GOD has declared you as HIS leader.

Here is the heart of JESUS as spoken through Paul in Ephesians 4:32 –

32 *Be kind and compassionate to one another, forgiving each other, just as in Christ God forgave you.*

GOD told us to forgive each other because HE wants us to mimic HIM. HE always has.

See People as GOD Sees Them

Speaking of the heart, here is what GOD sees when looking at a person.

1 Samuel 16:7b –

"For the Lord does not see as man sees; for man looks at the outward appearance, but the Lord looks at the heart."

Do you see potential in everyone? Each human was made special by GOD and HE gave each person a special gift.

GOD spoke through Peter's letter.

1 Peter 4:7 – 10 –

7 But the end of all things is at hand; therefore be serious and
watchful in your prayers. 8 And above all things have fervent love
for one another, for "love will cover a multitude of
sins." 9 Be hospitable to one another without grumbling. 10 As each
one has received a gift, minister it to one another, as good stewards
of the manifold grace of God.

Not every worker is a good fit for your business or job. But that should not stop you from loving everyone you meet.

I believe you have a special gift to reach people for CHRIST. Your gift is different than mine. If we all had the same gift, then only a few people could be reached. GOD wants everyone and it will take different people to reach everyone.

*Write how you will see people as special in your **Personal Ark**. Also write how you will pray for those who may no longer be a good fit for your company.*

Working with People Who Think Different Than Me

This page is from the *GOD-Centered Business: A Foundational Framework to Grow with Resilience.* Staying who you are is very important. If you are a shy person, forcing yourself to be gregarious is not recommended. Your personality and behaviors are what make you special and unique. There are people who need your style and GOD is willing to send them to you or you to them.

"**Be yourself**" is an action accepted by leaders. It means be confident to approach people just as you are. This does not mean you should not modify behaviors that may be harmful to others. It simply means be comfortable with your personality and appearance. GOD loves you and considers you wonderful!

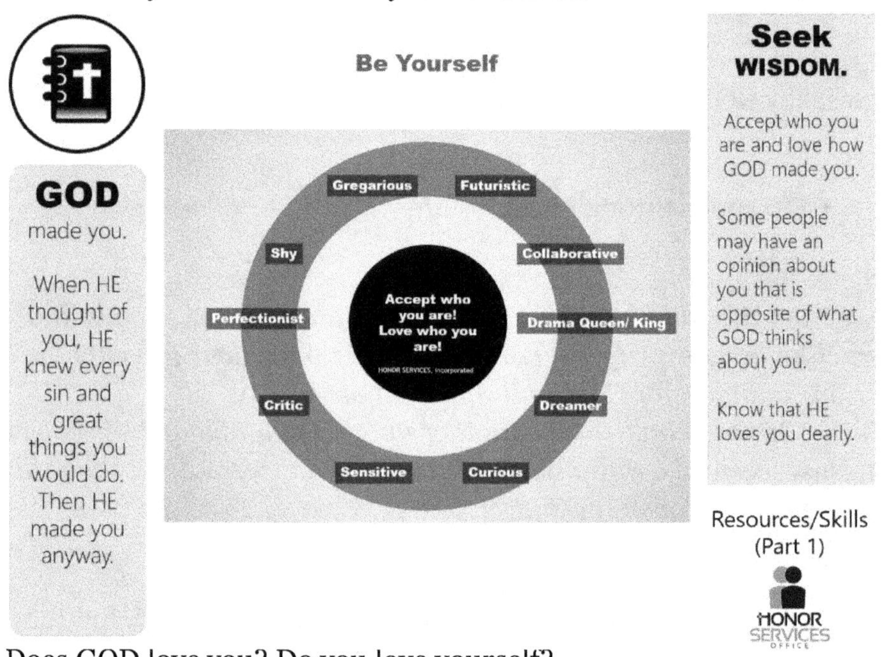

Does GOD love you? Do you love yourself?

Love and accept who you are. Review the image and identify a few behavioral traits that describe who you are.

GOD was pleased when HE made you. Some people may have a different opinion about you, but GOD thinks you are wonderful! The first step to loving you is to accept your behaviors. Look at the image and identify one or more behaviors that describe how you behave sometimes. *Write your observations in your **Personal Ark**.*

Comparison Trap Affects Your Pace

One trap many leaders fall into is comparison. When you fall into this trap, your mind quickly conjures up False Evidence Appearing Real (FEAR). This makes you prone to rumor versus the facts that you have worked so hard for. Here are a few consequences of comparing yourself to other people.

Prone to be taken off the vision – People who try to take you off your destination may sometimes place tactics in front of you and make you feel your life is incomplete without using the tactic. Think strategically. A strategy will not change, but the tactic will.

Example: A marketing strategy may be "Host an Event." A tactic used in the past to gain awareness was to print half sheets of paper with a nice design and stand in a populated area, handing out the paper. This evolved to a tactic of posting information on "listing boards" such as Craigslist. This evolved into social media posting. But the strategy of "Host an Event" never changed.

Groups can also pull you off of your destination. Volunteer groups who are strapped for volunteers may place demands on you that are above and beyond what you can offer. Be a leader and contribute what you can. *Write how you will stay focused on your vision in your* ***Personal Ark***.

Open to overloading the calendar – When I see an overloaded calendar, I see a person who may be experiencing FEAR due to lack of confidence. **You control the pace**. Mimicking GOD is what we should do. HE slows us down when we are moving too fast and speeds us up when we should be moving with fervor.

If you are burned out or people on your team are worn down, it may be due to you not controlling the pace to the current capacity GOD has give you. Be brave enough to say **No** to events and **Yes** to leaving gaps on your calendar. FEAR will make the event look important, but **the fruit of the SPIRIT gives you self-control**. *Write how you will control the pace and add gaps on your calendar in your* ***Personal Ark.***

Despising the current size of your business – The last thing I see when people compare themselves to other people is them not liking or appreciating where they are. To get "big" you must **dream big while acting small.**

Zechariah 4:10a –

"Do not despise these small beginnings, for the LORD rejoices to see the work begin,"

GOD is excited that you said yes! Obedience to HIS calling is your measurement. Comparing yourself to someone's size, wealth or ease in which they can do things could make you think your efforts are less than what they really are. To GOD, the first step is huge and so are the steps that follow.

Celebrities, large churches and large companies make everything look easy and cost less. Meanwhile, your costs may be higher because you don't have the income levels as larger firms. This calls for you to think about your **thankful differentiators** you thought of in visioning. **GOD will send people to you because of you**, not your copy of a large group or the latest tactic. Be yourself!

They may be too big for their own good. Many large organizations cannot provide the care and customer service that you can.

Rewrite your thankful differentiators in your ***Personal Ark***. See the *Dream Bigger* section of the *GOD-Centered Business: A Foundational Framework to Grow with Resilience* for more insights about thankfulness.

Let's look at someone who was not afraid of being herself. She was going to succeed, despite facing being killed.

Bravery of a Mother

Caring, protecting and seeing what GOD sees in people is exactly what Jochebed did when she made the ark for Moses.

Jochebed was Moses's mother. Before Moses was born, a Pharaoh declared that all male babies must be killed by throwing them in the river.

Exodus 1:15 – 18 –

*15 Then the king of Egypt spoke to the Hebrew midwives, of
whom the name of one was Shiphrah and the name of the other
Puah; 16 and he said, "When you do the duties of a midwife for the
Hebrew women, and see them on the birthstools, if it is a son, then
you shall kill him; but if it is a daughter, then she shall live." 17 But
the midwives feared God, and did not do as the king of Egypt
commanded them, but saved the male children alive. 18 So the king
of Egypt called for the midwives and said to them, "Why have you
done this thing, and saved the male children alive?"*

Exodus 1:22 –

22 So Pharaoh commanded all his people, saying, "Every son who is born you shall cast into the river, and every daughter you shall save alive."

Amram, Moses's father and Jochebed also feared the LORD in a healthy way. After they got married, they had a child. Jochebed saw something special in her child. She created a **Personal Ark** to care and protect Moses. Jochebed's ark is rarely preached.

Exodus 2:1 – 4 –

And a man of the house of Levi went and took as wife a
daughter of Levi. 2 *So the woman conceived and bore a son.*
And when she saw that he was a beautiful child, she hid him three
months. 3 *But when she could no longer hide him, she took an ark*
of bulrushes for him, daubed it with asphalt and pitch, put the child
in it, and laid it in the reeds by the river's bank. 4 *And his sister*
stood afar off, to know what would be done to him.

Observation 1: Jochebed saw something special in Moses.

My first observation is Jochebed saw something special in Moses. As a parent, I think my children are special as many parents do. But there was something extremely special about Moses. Almost like an anointing from GOD that could be seen. Miriam and Aaron were Moses's siblings. They were also special to Amram and Jochebed, but GOD had a special mission for Moses that his parents could not understand. What do you see in people?

GOD does not show HIS plan to us all at once. HE shows us little pieces of HIS plan a little at a time so we can understand. HE did not tell Moses's parents what HE had in store for him. They acted on faith. *Write how you will look for something special in everyone in your* ***Personal Ark****.*

Your world opens up when you see more people as special to GOD. Somehow the brief interaction you have with people is important to HIM. We have the opportunity to make the most out of every interaction. When the HOLY SPIRIT prompts you, maybe smile on purpose or pray for the stranger. GOD sees when you recognize people as special to HIM.

Observation 2: Jochebed cared for Moses more than her own life.

My next observation is that Jochebed cared for Moses. For three months, she hid him. This means every time Moses wanted to cry, she was able to slip away from her duties and nurse him or tend to his needs. She risked her life by hiding him, but that did not matter as long as Moses remained alive.

A mother's love is amazing and special! Every day she could have been caught and executed because she did not follow what Pharaoh said. But after three months of hiding him, Jochebed had to give Moses over to GOD. She could not hide him as easily. Are you willing to take a risk to care for others? *Write how you will intentionally care for people in your* ***Personal Ark***.

Caring takes energy, so use wisdom and discernment to choose people who will do the work wisely. Ask questions about their capabilities, but also get to know the person. You are on your way to building a skilled community. Did the person you just met complain a lot? How about the opposite – did the person compliment you too much?

You are the leader who received the vision for your business from GOD. No one knows your business better than you.

Observation 3: Jochebed wanted to protect Moses as best she could.

My third observation is Jochebed wanted to protect Moses as best as she could. Jochebed built an ark out of bulrushes basket material. I believe this was not a normal basket; rather, it was shaped differently. It was a little ark. She wanted to protect Moses from Pharaoh so she made a top to conceal him. She also wanted to protect Moses from wild animals.

She made the ark able to float. She added asphalt and pitch to the bulrushes. This vessel was not made for a long journey. It only had room for one three-month-old baby. There was no food mentioned or a change of clothes. Only Moses.

Jochebed could no longer hide Moses. She wanted him to live so she placed him in the ark and possibly hoped and prayed that GOD would do something to protect him. She was right!

She sent his sister Miriam to watch over him as the ark floated down the Nile River. How are you protecting the people GOD has put in your life? Even your enemies. *Write how you will protect people even those who may not have your best interest in mind in your **Personal Ark**.*

Standing up for those who work for you will go a long way. They can feel when you are protecting them. Conversely, they can also feel when you are blaming them or throwing them under the bus. It takes time to build a relationship of protection and trust. Are you willing to immediately give this caring and trust away to someone you just met?

Take a moment to think about all the people who used to work for you or with you. If you have experienced a high amount of turnover, then it could be because of a lack of clarity or them feeling like you will not care for them or protect them.

Be careful not to take on too much responsibility for their performance. Remember, you vetted each worker based on the **Purpose Ark** you wrote for them. You wrote the **Purpose Ark** for a reason, namely to get the work done. Warn the underperformer before severing ties. If you find yourself severing ties often, then, perhaps adjust the **Purpose Ark** for clarity and your **Personal Ark** for how to work with people.

Observation 4: GOD needed to intervene.

My last observation is about GOD. HE does wonderful remarkable things when we surrender to HIM. This situation seemed impossible. Moses's chance of survival was zero. He could not do anything for himself or save himself. His mother made an ark out of bulrushes and put him inside. She closed the lid and put the ark on the water. How was this flimsy plan supposed to work?

GOD was the factor that made the impossible plan work!

Exodus 2: 5 – 10 –

5 Then the daughter of Pharaoh came down to bathe at the
river. And her maidens walked along the riverside; and when she
saw the ark among the reeds, she sent her maid to get it. 6 And
when she opened it, she saw the child, and behold, the baby wept.
So she had compassion on him, and said, "This is one of the
Hebrews' children."

7 Then his sister said to Pharaoh's daughter, "Shall I go and
call a nurse for you from the Hebrew women, that she may nurse
the child for you?"

8 And Pharaoh's daughter said to her, "Go." So the maiden
went and called the child's mother. 9 Then Pharaoh's daughter said
to her, "Take this child away and nurse him for me, and I will
give you your wages." So the woman took the child and nursed
him. 10 And the child grew, and she brought him to Pharaoh's
daughter, and he became her son. So she called his name Moses,
saying, "Because I drew him out of the water."

GOD gave Jochebed her child back! She gave him to GOD and HE gave him back! Jochebed, Moses's mom, gave Moses, her son, over to GOD, and HE gave him back! You can tell I am excited! Pharaoh's daughter saw that the baby was Hebrew, possibly because he was circumcised. She sent for a Hebrew woman to nurse the baby and Miriam, Moses's sister, chose their mother to be the one. Jochebed's flimsy plan worked because GOD made it work.

Moses was pulled from the water or saved from the water as his name indicates. He was raised by the Egyptian family who made the decree to kill all Hebrew male babies. GOD seems to have a sense of humor here. But it says a lot. GOD can and will make your enemies bear the burdens of supporting you when they meant evil over you.

enemy - a person, group, or nation actively hostile, opposing, or seeking to injure another

Satan is “the Enemy”

Jochebed was not looking for her enemy, Pharaoh, to support her; so, you should not wait on your enemies to suddenly support you. Let GOD work on the situation without needing to see enemy conversions. How are you believing GOD to handle this situation? *Write the situation you need to place total trust in GOD in your **Personal Ark**.*

Believing that GOD will deliver you is easy on the first day; but what happens if days turns into weeks or months or years? Your belief in GOD cannot be measured by likes on social media or how well you are known. Your only measurement is whether or not you said, “Yes!” **Your obedience is your only measurement**.

You may be tempted to ask GOD questions like, “How, why, where, what, or when?” because of doubts or worries. But when GOD said for you to do something for HIS people, and you obey, HIS promise is sealed for you. HE promised HE would reward you and you can place your trust in knowing that HE keeps HIS promises.

What promises are you making to GOD? What promises are you making to your customers, workers and family? Are you brave enough to admit you do not know when GOD will reward you, but you will remain faithful until HE does?

*Write down GOD’s promises for you in your **Personal Ark**.*

Surrender and Trust

Surrender and trust are what I see here. Jochebed could not go any further with the plan of hiding Moses. She saw something special in him and cared for him but had to take her hands off of him and let GOD do as HE wished. She did not give up; rather, she surrendered. This plan had failure written all over it. Come on, a baby in an ark made out of bulrushes? That's the plan!? Yes! Have you ever had your back against the wall and had to rely totally on GOD to deliver you out of the situation?

GOD sees something special in you. HE cares for you. HE protects you. HE can use your plan that you think is pitiful, and make it work. HE wants you to see people the same as Jochebed saw Moses. Do you see people as being special to GOD? Are people only employees or are they people? How are you protecting people? Do you need to release your control so GOD can protect the people as only HE can?

Now that you see that GOD cares about you and protects you and sees something special inside you, HE wants you to make adjustments in yourself to work with other people.

Adjust Yourself

Working with others takes effort. Whether customers or employees, each person is different. See if you need to make some minor adjustments to reach people while staying in your comfort zone.

In the chart below and in the following pages from the *GOD-Centered Business: A Foundational Framework to Grow with Resilience,* identify your behaviors and the suggestions for interacting with other people.

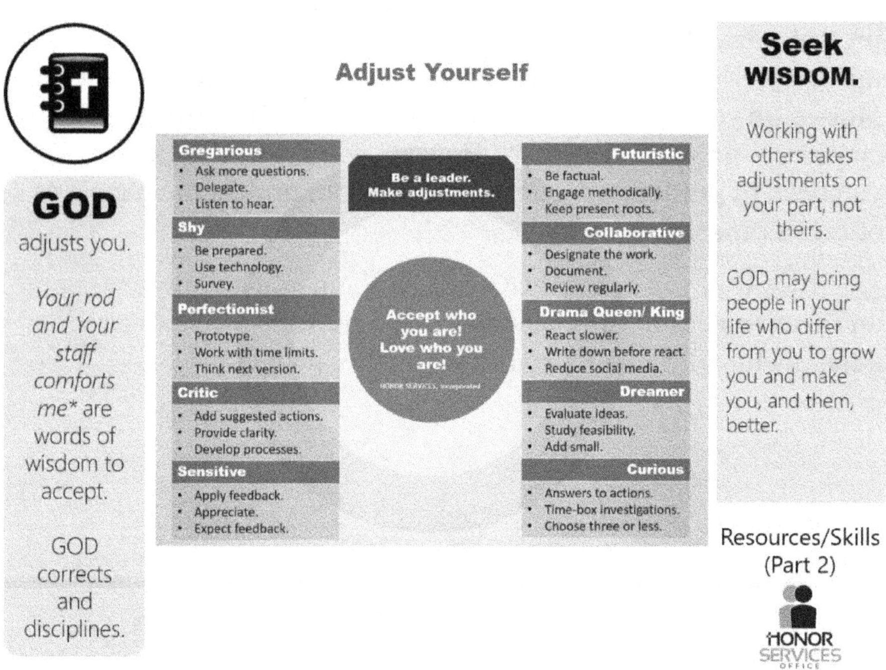

Have you ever met someone who just rubbed you the wrong way? I mean, they just got on your nerves. Is it hard to listen to that person? What if that person was saying something valuable to you that you needed to hear? Would you close your ears to what they had to say?

GOD adjusts us.

Psalm 23:4 –

Yea, though I walk through the valley of the shadow of death, I will fear no evil; For You are with me; Your rod and Your staff, they comfort me.

GOD gently corrects us with HIS rod of truth. This brings comfort.

Know Yourself to Make Adjustments

When engaging with workers, potential customers or clients, know yourself and make adjustments on how you approach people. Look at the list below and identify an approach to how you will meet people.

Behavior	Strengths	Opportunities	Suggested Approach(es)
Futuristic (aka the Innovator)	Visionary, innovative, imaginative, inventive	May move to the next thing too quickly, sometimes speaks without facts, may be discontented	Be factual. Engage with a methodology rather than winging it. Spend a balanced time in the present and in the future.
Collaborative	Brings people together; energized by groups; serves people	May miss details by talking and not documenting or by being involved in all conversations; puts people over process once too often	Delegate the work. Keep conversations short but meaningful. Document needs. Review processes with those you are working with.

Working with People Who Think Different Than Me

Behavior	Strengths	Opportunities	Suggested Approach(es)
Dreamer	Imaginative; likes big ideas; visionary; solutions driven	Sometimes thinks all ideas are good ideas; may skip testing or may take on too much and not deliver	Evaluate ideas and test before implementing. Study feasibility. Break ideas up into smaller implementable pieces.
Drama Queen/ King	Excited; passionate; enjoys the spotlight (center of attention)	May react without asking for clarification, speaks before thinking; often posts irrelevant information on social media	React slower. Write responses after a 24-hour cool down period. Reduce social media posts to relevant information only.
Curious	Inquisitive; research driven; factual	Prone to over-analyze; looks for problems where there may not be any; presents too many options to customers	Timebox investigations. Provide answers only to problems given to you. Choose two or three solutions to present.
Sensitive	Empathetic; understanding, reads nonverbals	Adverse to feedback; withholds improvements; may boil over and lash out	Seek feedback on regular intervals versus whenever you feel like it. Expect and accept feedback as a gift. Add appreciation.

Trust Is My New Skill
Building a Skilled Community

Behavior	Strengths	Opportunities	Suggested Approach(es)
Critical	Solves problems; looks for root cause; provides improvements.	May provide too many improvements than others can handle; can come off as abrasive; never seems satisfied	Bring others in on solutions and accept their ideas. Delegate improvements and inspections. Accept the pace of others with patience.
Perfectionist	Likes high quality; high performance; high standards	May take longer than needed or expected; frustrated easily by mistakes; comes across as hard to please	Develop prototypes to get feedback, rather than waiting on finished product. Work timebound. Think of putting improvements in the next version.
Shy	Great listener; observant, thinker/ intellect	May feel uncomfortable speaking to strangers who can grow the business; may overthink what others are thinking based on insecurities; may look for self-fulfilling failure	Be prepared and use technology to focus the audience's attention away from you. Focus more on the valuable message needing to be heard by the receiver, thus relieving him or her of a problem.

Working with People Who Think Different Than Me

Behavior	Strengths	Opportunities	Suggested Approach(es)
Gregarious	Meets new people easily; public speaker; has a host of prepared messages and wisdom to impart	May speak before listening; takes over the conversation; may not seek input	Ask more questions. Listen to hear. Delegate to others. Seek advice before giving it.

Insecurities and self-doubt could prevent you from giving a valuable message to the person who needs to hear it. On the other hand, speaking at people rather than hearing their needs creates a situation where the speaker could miss out on what is needed to be said. How can you adjust how you speak to people? *Write your adjustments in your* ***Personal Ark****.*

Again, GOD made you wonderfully and is pleased with you. Use the gifts and talents HE gave you to grow HIS kingdom through your business. HE is excited and has a plan for you!

Working with strangers takes humility that only comes from GOD correcting us, sometimes gently, sometimes harder than we'd like. Self-control is the only control worth seeking. This is a part of the fruit of the Spirit. *Write adjustments you will make to work with people who look and act differently than you do in your* ***Personal Ark***. Now let's adjust the mood of a leader.

Seek a Better Mood

Your mood affects your business. Each day, the GOD-Centered Business owner will need to choose how to approach the day. The images that follow are from the *GOD-Centered Business: A Foundational Framework to Grow with Resilience.*

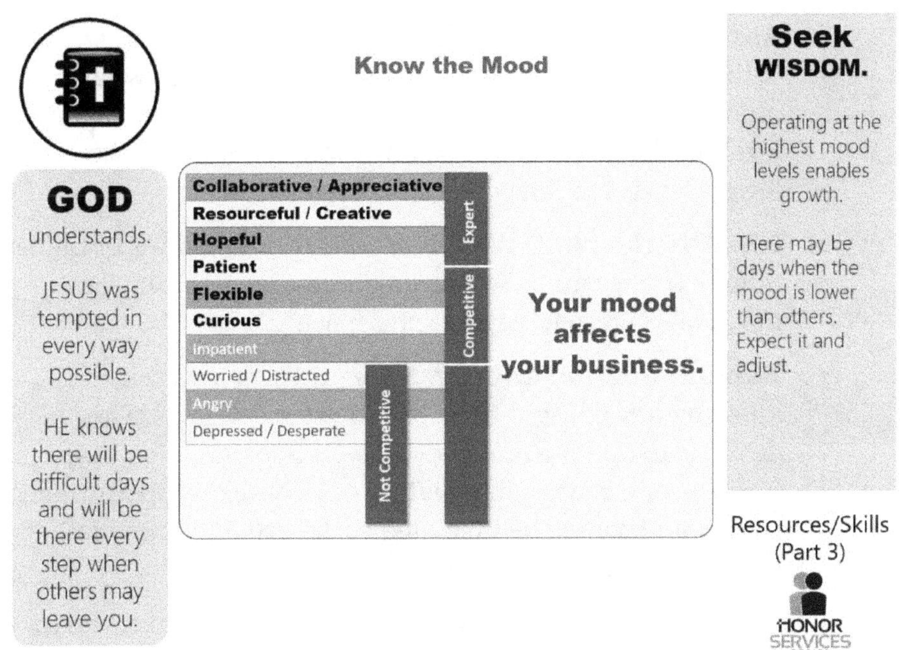

Have you ever met someone who just lights up the room? I mean their very presence makes everyone smile even though they haven't said a word? On the flip side, have you ever met someone who seems to work bad or negative news into every conversation? Can you recognize when someone is sad?

Their mood shows up on their face. Yours does too. Do you ever assess your mood? What is the mood of your business? The mood of the business will affect the performance of the business. JESUS understands having a bad day.

Expect to operate in the lower moods every now and then, but do not stay there. What do you notice about the image? The higher moods showcase your expertise.

Write down the mood of your business as part of your ***Personal Ark***.

1. **Assess your mood.** Before self-examination or quiet time with the LORD, purposefully and honestly check what mood you are in. You cannot always operate at the highest levels of the mood elevator; however, operating at the lowest levels too long can cause exhaustion.
2. **Identify the root.** What is the cause of the lower or higher mood? Higher mood levels enable **praise** while lower mood levels trigger **prayer**. Be specific.
3. **Expend healthy energy.** Have grace for yourself, knowing it is all right to be in a lower mood level. The desire is to operate at a higher level. Depending on other humans or a change in situation can cause disappointment. GOD wants you to be insulated with permanent joy, rather than temporary happiness.

By being honest about moods and identifying what put you in this mood, you can give GOD praise or surrender the issue to HIM. Giving GOD praise may come harder for those who need to feel wanted and desire attention. Surrender may be difficult for those who have been in a lower mood for an extended time and have no energy to do anything. In either case, you may need help from those skilled in guiding people to operate in higher levels in a godly way.

GOD is GOD and we are humans. It is alright for us to have emotions and up and down moods. HE does not need us to try harder or to be GOD. HE simply wants us to follow HIS leading.

Adjust the Mood

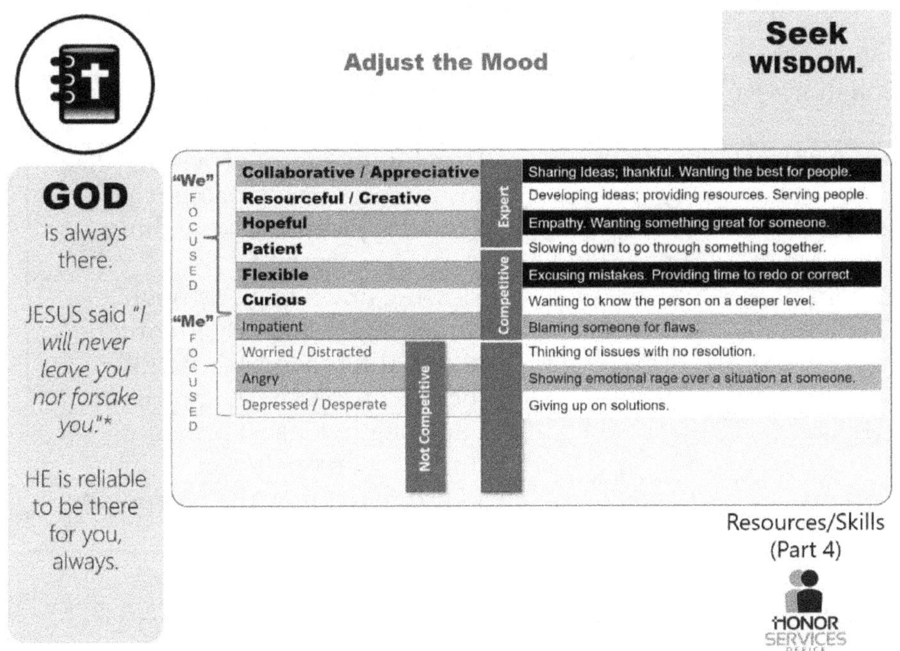

Have you ever been let down when you expected someone to come through for you?

GOD's promises are never broken. HE will always be there for you.

Hebrews 13:5 –
Make sure that your character is free from the love of money, being content with what you have; for He Himself has said, "I WILL NEVER DESERT YOU, NOR WILL *I* EVER FORSAKE YOU, (NASB) (or) *Let your conduct be without covetousness; be content with such things as you have. For He Himself has said, "I will never leave you nor forsake you. (NKJV)*

GOD never leaves you. This comforting and reassuring message can help you.

Operating at Higher Mood Levels

Operating at higher mood level is usually "**we focused**."

Higher Mood	Description
Collaborative/Appreciative	Sharing ideas; thankful; wanting the best for people
Resourceful/Creative	Developing ideas; providing resources; serving people
Hopeful	Empathy; wanting something great for someone
Patient	Slowing down to go through something together with others; taking time to include quality; increase proactive responses
Flexible	Excusing mistakes; providing time to redo or correct
Curious	Wanting to know the person on a deeper level

GOD made you wonderful, gave you purpose and has great plans for you! Don't you want this for other people? When your day starts with the right mood, you can see other people easier. "It's about us" versus "It's about me." GOD made you an ambassador and is raising you up. HE does not want you to carry HIS load, but rather to share in the rewards of being faithful to HIM.

HE knows you will have some days that are better than others. Knowing where your mood is helps you regulate it so you can work within the higher mood levels. Here is a Bible passage that helps me let go of what GOD should be carrying.

Matthew 11:28 – 30 –

28 *Come unto me, all ye that labour and are heavy laden, and I will give you rest.*

29 *Take my yoke upon you, and learn of me; for I am meek and lowly in heart: and ye shall find rest unto your souls.*

30 *For my yoke is easy, and my burden is light.* (KJV)

Operating at Lower Mood Levels

Operating at lower mood levels can be "**me focused**."

Lower Mood	Description	Suggestion
Impatient	Blaming others for their flaws does not fix the situation. This can cause the recipient to lose courage.	Seek patience little by little with this person and others. Also, be patient with yourself.
Worried or Distracted	Thinking of issues with no resolution over and over can cause a state of worry.	Schedule a day and time to consider the issue and possible ways to approach a resolution. This way you can **rest** and not replay the issue. Say, "I will think about that on Thursday at 2:00 PM."
Angry or Sad	Getting emotional over a situation increases the possibility of harming self or others.	Emotional intelligence is used to rationally control harmful emotions. Seek help if these emotions cannot be controlled. Use the fruit of the Spirit, self-control to manage emotions.
Depressed / Desperate	Giving up on all solutions increases the desire to work or be alone, thus leaving one susceptible to increased negative thoughts.	Fight the urge to be alone and surround yourself with praying people. Seek help from someone who is skilled in guiding people to operate in higher levels in a godly way.

Working with People Who Think Different Than Me

Not every day will be easy. Knowing where you are in your mood level helps you seek help from GOD and other people. If you are asking the question, "What about me?" just know it is alright to ask that question. GOD hears you and cares for you.

But when operating in lower moods too long, it is imperative to meet with people who can open your eyes to the root cause of the negativity so you can get to a place where you can hear GOD again.

For some, it may take a professional who is skilled in bringing people to higher mood levels. For others, a wise, prayerful person who listens well might be the answer. This is a great time for prayer and surrender to GOD.

When operating in higher mood levels, it is imperative to meet the people to whom GOD wants you to speak, bringing them along, growing them, and serving them. Higher or positive moods bring positive results. This is a great time of praise.

Days when I am afraid, I read this passage.
Joshua 1:7 – 9 –

7 *"Be strong and very courageous. Be careful to obey all the law my servant Moses gave you; do not turn from it to the right or to the left, that you may be successful wherever you go.*
8 *Keep this Book of the Law always on your lips; meditate on it day and night, so that you may be careful to do everything written in it. Then you will be prosperous and successful.*
9 *Have I not commanded you? Be strong and courageous. Do not be afraid; do not be discouraged, for the Lord your God will be with you wherever you go."*

Days when I am overwhelmed, I read this passage.

Isaiah 41:10 –

10 *Don't be afraid, for I am with you.*
Don't be discouraged, for I am your God.
I will strengthen you and help you.
I will hold you up with my victorious right hand.

Days when I feel like giving up, I read this passage.

Romans 5:3 – 4 –

3 And not only that, but we also glory in tribulations, knowing that tribulation produces perseverance; 4 and perseverance, character; and character, hope.

Days when I am uncertain, I read this verse.

Deuteronomy 31:8 –

The LORD himself goes before you and will be with you; he will never leave you nor forsake you. Do not be afraid; do not be discouraged. (NIV)

This is not a time to try harder or be more than GOD calls you to be. If you are disappointed with current results, you may get disappointed with GOD, thinking HE has left you. HE is right there. Take GOD's yoke. This means let HIM do HIS work and your part will be easy.

Remember, if you are D-E-A-D (desperate expecting acquisitive dollars) you will always sound dead. We are ALIVE! Appreciative, Loving, Inviting, Victorious, and Everlasting.

Put work away and get rest. Wake up and go into your day with a planned mood. Expect difficulties and plan how you will handle them beforehand.

Working in the higher mood levels takes practice. Some days it will be harder than others to work in the higher moods, but return to the mood image monthly to assess how you are performing in this vital area.

*Write activities you will perform to work in the higher mood levels more often in your **Personal Ark**.*

Who do you like hanging out with in your industry? Are there certain customers you know who will give you some great feedback as well as new ideas? Are there people you are thankful for?"

Fill in the responses to the following questions to set the mood for your business and update your ***Personal Ark****.*

Who do I collaborate with?

Who do I appreciate and value?

Who do I go to for ideas and who can I provide ideas to?

What issues should I be more flexible on?

Am I getting enough rest by stepping away from thinking about work?

Who do I want to get to know more so eventually I can share my experiences with GOD with them?

Confidence should be placed in GOD making you exactly as HE needs you. HE equipped you with everything you need to be successful in HIS calling on your life. Even when it does not seem like things are going well, GOD's calling on your life is going exactly according to plan. HE made you HIS leader and has your back. After you fight HIM and tell HIM, "No, I don't want to lead," HE will await your Yes and will then equip you for leading HIS people.

Your **Personal Ark** should have a lot of information in it by now. You have listed how you will care, protect and recognize what GOD values in people. You have written how you will stay away from comparing yourself to other people and companies. You also have written how you will adjust yourself to work with people and work at the higher mood levels. Let's seek a skilled community by seeking GOD's Kingdom.

WARNING

- Check to see if your leadership style wants people to remain under you. You should want the best for people and want them to grow beyond your leadership.
- Be careful not to stray too far from the **Purpose Arks** you have defined. When resources pop up, realize they can unknowingly take you away from your destination by placing a shiny new object in front of you that may derail you and cause more effort to get back on track.

NEXT STEPS

- Address leadership qualities that you may not like about yourself by doing a self-examination.
- Slow down when it comes to bringing on employees, volunteers, and contractors. Understand each person's capabilities to see if they are a match for the purpose you have defined.
- Get to know people before making too many adjustments. Trying to get people to behave differently will take you making self-adjustments, versus telling other people how to behave. Model behaviors you want others to embrace.

Do I have to work with others?

Build a Persuasive Ark to Work with Others

Gravitating to people who leaned more towards being level-headed came from me being bullied. I was malnourished, not because my parents did not try to feed me, but because I did not like food. I did not want anything with fat on it, no fish, hated cheesy stuff and despised most candy and deserts. Oh yeah, fruit was disgusting and so were vegetables!

Being a picky eater contributed to my small stature. What took someone with muscles one pull took me seven. Before I learned to get some help doing things; when something got hard to accomplish, I would try seven times harder than the next person and would sometimes be rewarded for my tenacity. But the bigger accomplishments required that I work with people.

Leadership Tip #5 – Working by yourself leaves you open to acting on things without confirmation from the people GOD provides.

Being on a team is one thing, but leading a team is another. "But I work alone," you may say. You may work with more people than you think. Consider valuing external resources as your team.

The last ark I will focus on is the Ark of the Covenant. This ark was so powerful that if touched incorrectly, the person would die. This ark was made by Bezalel with Moses as the orchestrator and was used to keep everyone encouraged when facing trials. Your **Purpose Ark** and **Personal Ark** will be needed to build your **Persuasive Ark**.

Building a Persuasive Ark is a process to document how you will courageously grow a community that you influence to use their hard and soft skills to build, operate, and grow other people and your business, overcoming obstacles and trials, to make it profitable for the ultimate purpose of growing and thriving in GOD's Kingdom.

You may believe in the purpose of your product or service. You may have prepared yourself to be the expert. But how do you persuade people to do the work necessary to make your business or job successful when **facing life's difficulties**? It will take your influence.

Let's look at an image from the *GOD-Centered Business: A Framework to Grow with Resilience*, that could be a model of your business.

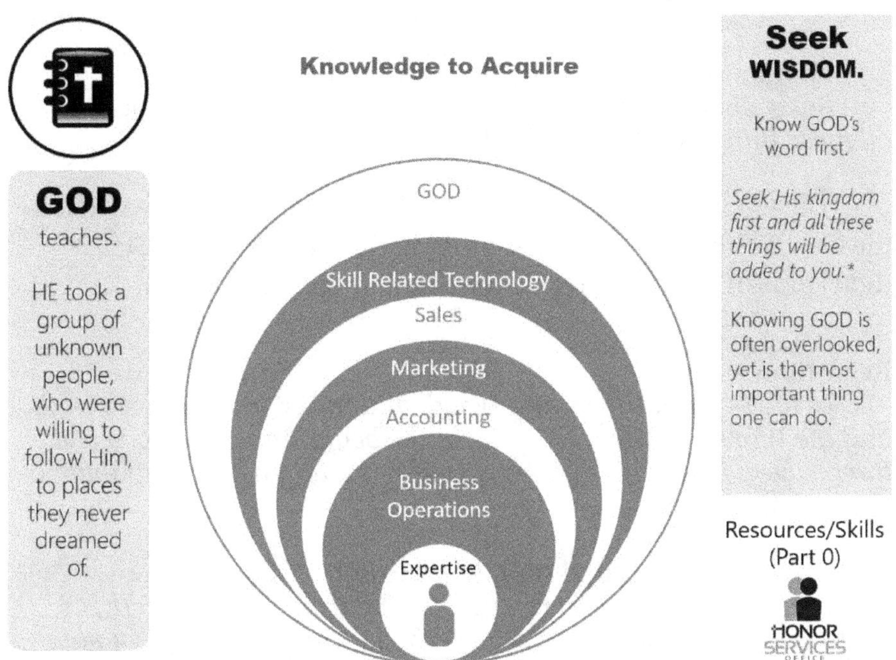

The inner ring represents your expertise. The next ring is Business Operations, then Accounting, then Marketing, then Sales, then some Skill Related Technology all inside the ring which is GOD.

Working within GOD takes you to get to know HIM and that takes reading the Bible for yourself to understand who HE is by what HE revealed. I believe in the S.O.A.P. method for reading the Bible. Read the **S**-Scripture, write down your **O**-Observation, make it personal by **A**-Applying it to your life and **P**-Pray about what you read. Have a conversation in your prayer with GOD, asking HIM to reveal the meaning and application.

Be consistent. Try to read daily for at least 36 days. In the *GOD-Centered Business: A Foundational Framework to Grow with Resilience*, there is a *36-Day Devotional* to start you on your journey to self-discover CHRIST.

Working with People Who Think Different Than Me

Have you ever liked someone enough to find out more about him or her? Did you ask questions to them or talk to their friends? GOD wants to be known. By seeking GOD, HE will teach you and add the right things you need.

Matthew 6:33 –
But seek first the kingdom of God and His righteousness, and all these things shall be added to you.

Let's look at two sections of the Bible. One scripture written in the New Testament and one written in the Old Testament, thousands of years before the New Testament was written.

Read John 1:1-3 –
In the beginning was the Word, and the Word was with God, and the Word was God. He was in the beginning with God. All things were made through Him, and without Him nothing was made that was made.

Now read Genesis 1:1 and compare it to John 1:1-3.
In the beginning God created the heavens and the earth.
What similarities do you notice? *Write your observations in your **Persuasive Ark**.*

Read John 1:1-5, 9-14 and **circle** the references to JESUS.

The Eternal Word
1 In the beginning was the Word, and the Word was with
God, and the Word was God. 2 He was with God in the
beginning. 3 Through him all things were made; without him
nothing was made that has been made. 4 In him was life, and that
life was the light of all mankind. 5 The light shines in the
darkness, and the darkness has not overcome it.

9 The true light that gives light to everyone was coming into
the world. 10 He was in the world, and though the world was made
through him, the world did not recognize him. 11 He came to that
which was his own, but his own did not receive him. 12 Yet to all
who did receive him, to those who believed in his name, he gave the
right to become children of God— 13 children born not of natural
descent, nor of human decision or a husband's will, but born of
God.
14 The Word became flesh and made his dwelling among us.
We have seen his glory, the glory of the one and only Son, who
came from the Father, full of grace and truth.

What do you observe about the role of the Word? *Write your observations in your* ***Persuasive Ark***.

Did anything stand out to you? If so, then write this down. What words seem to jump off the page at you? Remember them.

Let GOD measure your success. Allow HIM to guide you while obeying HIS direction. After getting your observations from daily reading, you will notice your day becoming more relaxed, even when storms come into your life. This is the first part of gaining clarity. Now you are ready to look at your team.

Team Member to Consider – Prayer Partner

"But it's just me," you may say. If you are working alone or if you have a team and you are the leader who feels alone, then there may be a person or people missing from your life. You may be missing a prayer partner. **Prayer is the most important conversation you can have in your life**. People label meetings with humans who have wealth as being important, but downgrade a conversation with GOD as mundane or powerless.

Prayer is sometimes considered a last resort, versus a strategic move. Prayer gets rid of fear, worry and doubt. We can ask GOD, who owns everything, for literally anything. HE may say, "No," but we can ask HIM for any and everything under the sun.

GOD wants to be your leader.

Jeremiah 30:22 –

[22] *'You shall be My people,*
And I will be your God.' "

Being GOD means HE will act different than a human. HE can stand being asked for clarity, but HE also is GOD and should not be treated as common. HE decided to interact with humans on an invitation only basis. HE does not force HIS way into our lives.

GOD waits on us to ask versus handing us everything we want. When we have to ask GOD into the plan, we submit ourselves to being told "Yes" or "No" or "Wait." This level of surrender should give us peace that the MOST HIGH GOD will listen to you and me.

Revelation 3:20 –

Behold, I stand at the door and knock. If anyone hears My voice and opens the door, I will come in to him and dine with him, and he with Me.

GOD wants to enter our hearts, but will not move in unless invited. HE shows love by giving you free will to choose HIM or not. HE seems to do the same with our plans. GOD is our friend but HE is GOD. GOD forgives, but HE is GOD. GOD wants us to have the best, but HE is GOD. In other words, GOD has the final say. When we pray with someone, HE will join in and listen to the prayer.

JESUS said through HIS servant Matthew:

Matthew 18:20 –

20 For where two or three are gathered together in My name, I am there in the midst of them."

You need a prayer partner who can come alongside of you and ask GOD for things that align with HIS search for lost people who need to return to HIM. When you seek HIS Kingdom, HE will add the things you seek and need to you.

You will not need to develop a **Purpose Ark or Persuasive Ark** for your Prayer Partner, but you may want to update your **Personal Ark,** adding prayer as the method in with you will obtain clarity, direction and wait on the decisions to come from GOD.

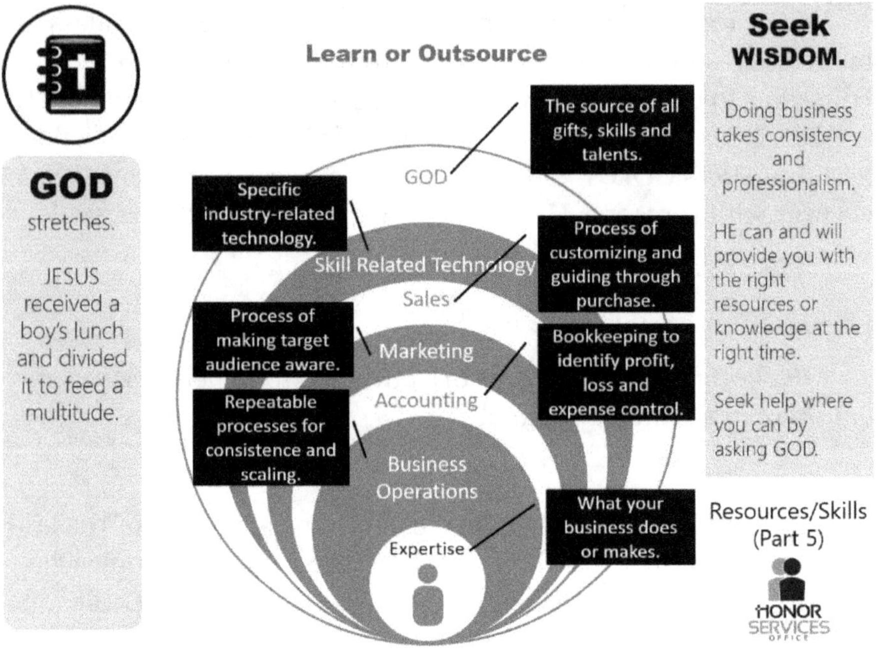

A decision has to be made for the remaining skills that I will discuss. "Should I learn this skill or outsource it?" is the question you should ask yourself for each skill I discuss. Take a look at this illustration from the *GOD-Centered Business: A Framework to Grow with Resilience*. In the *Seek Wisdom* section it guides you to make a decision to learn a skill or outsource.

While it may take up to five years of full-time effort to become an expert, you may become proficient enough at a skill to meet the needs of your business in a short time.

Learned Skill – A skill that will benefit your business that you become proficient enough to perform it at high achievement levels without underestimating or devaluing the difficulty level.

Outsourced Skill – A skill that someone performs because you do not possess the skill or do not have the bandwidth to perform it well. A word of caution. Outsourcing does not mean, throw it over the fence and let someone else do it. In other words, you must fully be aware of every aspect of the outsourced skill, so you know how to guide the expert in your customized need.

Here are some examples that you can use to develop and manage your **Purpose Ark** and **Personal Ark**.

Skill to Learn or Team Member to Consider – Business Operations

The necessary skill to develop written Standard Operating Procedures (SOPs) for yourself and others to follow to perform at a consistent level of excellence. Once you write an SOP, it can live as long as the procedure does not change. Usually, changes are made when the procedures are written are out versus when they are performed out of memory. Verify that the written steps work as expected.

In our cake baking example, an SOP would be written for baking cakes. Another would be created for cleaning and sanitation and another for raw material storage, rotation and handling.

*Develop a **Purpose Ark** for this role.*

Purpose Example: Your purpose is to create and manage the raw materials, baking and packaging processes.

Skills Needed Example: Food safety and raw material handling, SOP development and testing, waste reduction, inventory / rotation management, food cost management, cross-contamination management, people (roles), equipment and product (specifications), and health code management.

What You Should Expect Example: Written SOPs, Test Results, Revision Plans, Operations Metrics, Training Material, Validation Methods, Annual Safety Certificates, Annual Building Certificates, First Aid Procedures and Material Safety Data Sheets (MSDS), Theft and Fraud Prevention, Inventory Reports, Raw Material Orders, Waste Reports.

What do Business Operations look like for your industry? What standards do you have and which ones need consideration? Have you tested your standards on someone else? How can you pray for this person?

Skill to Learn or Team Member to Consider – Accounting

The necessary skill of keeping track of income, expenses and profit. This is your responsibility, not an accountant's. Why? You are the one who gives the accountant the correct information for them to do your taxes and other vital services. But you must be the one who understands all expenses and all income. You must also understand how to control expenses to maximize profit.

*Develop a **Purpose Ark** for this role.*

Purpose Example: Your purpose is to create and manage the budget, income / expense statements, quarterly payments and possibly payroll.

Skills Needed Example: Individual business, S-Corp, C-Corp, LLC tax knowledge; Profit and Loss (P&L) strategies, Pricing Strategies, Cost Reduction Strategies. Budgeting, Estimated Quarterly Payments.

What You Should Expect Example: Tax filings based on your itemized expenses, P&L Strategy, Pricing Strategy, Cost Strategy, Quarterly Payment Voucher, Budget.

What does financial management look like for your business? Are you categorizing your expenses? Are you using a pricing strategy? How should you adjust your budget?

Refer to the *GOD-Centered Business: A Foundational Framework to Grow with Resilience* in the *Emerge Different* section to understand pricing strategies.

Skill to Learn or Team Member to Consider – Marketing

The necessary skill of making people aware of your product and service to gain their trust in purchasing from your business. Trust is <u>earned</u>, and not easy to acquire. Getting certified in a particular skill or from a professional organization helps with awareness of your business, but does not prove you know how to operate the business to meet the needs of your customers. It only says you know how to do the skill.

*Develop a **Purpose Ark** for this role.*

Purpose Example: Your purpose is to create and manage the local store marketing (LSM), mass media, and social media marketing calendar.

Skills Needed Example: Knowledge of physical marketing such as signs, handouts and attractors to physical locations, mass media channels outside of social media and various social media techniques that increase capture rate versus solely getting views and likes. Some social media campaigns have been exploited by bots which can leave you with false results.

What You Should Expect Example: Marketing Calendar, LSM campaign, mass media campaign, social medial marketing campaign that accounts for bot attacks.

What does marketing look like for your product or service? Do you have a marketing calendar? How often are you putting items on sale? If too often, then the sale price becomes the price and you may lose profits. Who should be aware of your product or service?

Skill to Learn or Team Member to Consider – Sales

The necessary skill of leveraging a standard process for understanding the customer's needs, developing a deal that provides a "win-win" environment, guiding the person through the order and payment process and following up with promised goods and services and customer service after the purchase.

*Develop a **Purpose Ark** for this role.*

Purpose Example: Your purpose is to create and manage the various communities while providing our product. On-site visits are required.

Skills Needed Example: Sales process development, servant leadership, community development and management, deal development for large and small clients, order management and follow-up.

What You Should Expect Example: Sales process, products faced in retail spaces, individual contact notes and potential purchase rating, follow-up, deal structures, sample product, new clients and potential clients.

What communities should your business form? Are you B2B or B2C? How and when do you follow-up?

Skill to Learn or Team Member to Consider – Industry Technology

The necessary skill of knowing your industry. Most people feel very comfortable learning this because they like "doing" the business. Learn the skill while keeping GOD's Word in all aspects of your belief.

*Develop a **Purpose Ark** for this role.*

Purpose Example: Your purpose is to create and manage the onboarding, order taking/fulfilment, inventory, processes.

Skills Needed Example: Website Page Development, Access Security, Database Queries / Security, Payment Card Industry Compliance, Data Transport Security, eCommerce Workflow Knowledge, Broad Knowledge of Industries, Email Security and Workflow.

What you Should Expect Example: Website, Website Application, Secured Database, Workflows, Metrics.

What happens if the industry technology person leaves? What technology does your industry need? Can you perform the business without the industry technology? What is the technology that you use for your industry? The example above is for a tech company.

Decide to Learn or Outsource

*Write the skills you will learn or outsource in your **Persuasive Ark***. The goal is to operate the business, not just perform the expertise.

If you see a vital skill that you do not possess, do you automatically say, "I don't understand the missing skill, so I don't need the skill?"

What factors can you think of that cause a business to fail?

Some people may answer lack of money. This is far from the truth. A successful business starts with the vision from GOD who will guide them to people with a need. Fulfilling the needs of people with simple solutions and strong business practices enables GOD-Centered success.

How long do you think it will take to start or grow a business? Remember in “Remove the Trash” what a hurried business will do?

Many entrepreneurs don’t have time to develop good business practices, but have plenty of time to go out of business.

If you are missing a vital skill, will you ignore it or add this to your wish list to build a feature of your business?

How will the gap in a specific skill affect your timeline?

Write out a prayer for patience, wisdom and resources in your ***Persuasive Ark***. Pray for bravery to ask for help.

Let me give you some encouragement. “GOD will provide.” HE is the one who has you in business for HIS purpose. HE will equip you with the right skills or people. Also, pray for the helpers GOD sends to you. They are people too.

The Danger of Underestimating

Underestimating what a skill is or why it is needed is the business owner's or employer's downfall. I have seen many businesses underestimate the skill of technology, or marketing for example. In the example below we see a business owner who underestimates the skills truly needed to develop the app they wanted for their online business.

Skill Really Needed	Cousin Bud Says, "I can do it" capabilities
Website Page Development	Website Page Development
Access Security	~**Missing**~ Does not account for intruders
Database queries / security	~**Missing**~ Uses insecure methods to gather and store information
Payment Card Industry Compliance	~**Missing**~ Credit and Debit card information vulnerable causing fines
Data Transport Security	~**Missing**~ Middleman attacks easily implemented
eCommerce workflow knowledge	~**Missing**~ Complex shopping carts implemented without the company understanding the foundation
Broad range of industries	~**Missing**~ Uses extreme customization when an industry standard could be used
Email security and workflow	~**Missing**~ Hacked email or uses public email like Gmail causing limited contracts

GOD wants to help. Ask HIM for the missing skills instead of ignoring them.

Matthew 7:7 –

Ask, and it will be given to you; seek, and you will find; knock, and it will be opened to you.

Part of the **Personal Ark** is "trust." When GOD called you into business, it was not to make you fail. HE can and will provide.

Approaching missing skills as an opportunity rather than a barrier enables the GOD-Centered Business owner to meet many people of all walks of life. Not everyone has your best interest so be wise while seeking help.

Matthew 10:16 –

"Behold, I send you out as sheep in the midst of wolves. Therefore be wise as serpents and harmless as doves."

Getting help is important, but getting the right help is imperative. For example, JESUS's disciples asked GOD to help them choose another disciple when one was lost (see Acts 1:15-26).

Here are a few tips:

1. **Pray and ask GOD.** Seek GOD's answer to your skill gap. Be open to whomever HE sends or sends you to as a probable resource.

2. **Get references**. When outsourcing, ask for three references and follow up on the references. Check on the person's work so you can be sure he will provide the quality you are looking for.

3. **Pay your bills**. Immediately pay your workers and other resource people the agreed-upon price. You are worth your wages and so are they. Thank GOD for having the cash to be able to pay bills.

Now that we know who to work with or what skills to obtain, let's look at how we work with these people. It's time to begin building the **Persuasive Ark**.

Getting the work done at a high level of quality, on time and on budget is hard, but not impossible. It will take statements from your **Purpose Ark** to get the work started. But how do you track the work to completion? This will be part of your **Persuasive Ark.**

You must lead the development of your Business Features. I will go into detail about Business Features in another book because it is too extensive to describe here.

It will take influence to get the work done in a timely manner. People think money is the persuader, but have you heard horror stories of people who contracted with someone and they ran off with the money or did poor work? We want to prevent this from happening.

Remember your **Purpose Ark?** You defined the roles for each person on your team. This defined "why" the person was chosen, but does not define "how" the work will be done and "when" it will be accomplished.

If you are outsourcing a skill, I recommend that you get at least three bids for the work. This means you have to have the work defined clearly so the people can bid on the work. The more specific you can be, the better each bid will be. This will be done in a **Request for Proposal (RFP)** document. Without disclosing too much information, thus putting the bid together for the contractor, you will ask them to answer questions and provide estimates on clearly defined work.

Without describing "how" the work will be done, describe the problem you wish the skilled worker to perform. "Create Standard Operating Procedures for Cake Baking," is a good example of "what" needs to be done without describing "how" to do it.

Once you have chosen a contractor, worker or volunteer, it is now time to get the work fully defined and the payment schedule agreed upon.

You need to develop a **Statement of Work (SOW).** This is a formal document that discusses the scope of work, the time the work will be delivered and the cost/ resources needed. This document should have clear deliverables that are agreed upon. This document comes from your company, not theirs. **RFPs and SOWs are part of your Persuasive Ark.**

Host daily or weekly meetings to understand progress and what is left to do. But what happens when life hits and things do not go as planned? You are the leader who needs to keep everyone encouraged. Role by role, you will need to pray for each person to understand that GOD is here to help.

Persuasive Ark When Life Hits Hard

Having plans in place and people to execute the plans feels great at first. But expect things to go different than as planned. To put it mildly, you have an enemy who wants to stop you from reaching the destination GOD has in store for you.

Our team had just completed building a Business Feature. We tested the feature and it worked well. We got customers involved and made adjustments from their feedback. When we implemented the feature, things went well, at first. Before we could tell the world that we had new features, our hosting company sent a note stating, "A serious threat has been targeted all over the world. Take precaution." Additional development was needed to prevent the attack. This cost a lot more money and an additional six months!

Excitement we once had in nearing the finish line slowly dissipated. "Why now!?" was my question. You may have asked the same question when an additional expense pops up, or when someone gets upset and causes turmoil or even worse when someone is sick or a loved one passes away. What do you do when all of these problems hit at the same time?

Remember GOD's promises is something you can do.

Part of the **Persuasive Ark** is "**Overcoming obstacles and trials**." This is not a statement that says "pretend the problems don't exist" or "Ignore the problem" or "It's mentally your fault." What happens when you have done what you feel is right and problems still pop up? When your back is against the wall, **trust becomes the skill you rely on**. Let's look at some lessons that demonstrate leadership and community skills given to us through Moses's extremely difficult encounter with Pharaoh. I will use this situation as a case study you can use to increase your reliance on GOD's power.

Persuasive Ark to Remember GOD's Power

To understand the difficult situations you may experience, it is good to read how GOD brought people out of various difficulties. In this case study, I will look at the building of the Ark of the Covenant. But first let's look at how the people got into the difficult situation.

GOD heard the cry of HIS people in Egypt. They were slaves when times were good. Joseph, a leader in the Bible, was hated by his brothers, sold into slavery, thrown into prison while innocent and raised up to be a leader of Egypt. During his time, the people of Israel had it somewhat easy. But after he died, the Egyptians turned up their cruelty.

GOD helped HIS people leave Egypt from slavery HE told Moses to build the Ark of the Covenant to remember HE delivered them before and would continue to do it again.

GOD Sees Your Problems

After one pharaoh died another, fiercer, tyrant was put in his place. The people groaned because the work was so hard.

Exodus 3:7 – 10 –

7 And the Lord said: "I have surely seen the oppression of My people who are in Egypt, and have heard their cry because of their taskmasters, for I know their sorrows. 8 So I have come down to deliver them out of the hand of the Egyptians, and to bring them up from that land to a good and large land, to a land flowing with milk and honey, to the place of the Canaanites and the Hittites and the Amorites and the Perizzites and the Hivites and the Jebusites. 9 Now therefore, behold, the cry of the children of Israel has come to Me, and I have also seen the oppression with which the Egyptians oppress them. 10 Come now, therefore, and I will send you to Pharaoh that you may bring My people, the children of Israel, out of Egypt."

My first observation is **GOD sees your problems** before you cry out about it. HE sees the problems of those who had been mistreated, misunderstood and misguided.

When we face trials, we question GOD by asking, "Why?" We wiggle and squirm and tell people how much pain we are in. HE hears everything we say and has a plan of grace attached to the problem someone else caused. I do not like pain, but I am starting to understand it. If it were not because of pain, you would not be reading my words.

GOD provides us with a way out, but HE wants a testimony. Our testimony helps other people get through their situation without giving up. Your team needs to hear how to overcome the trial versus you saying, "Woe is me; everything is bad." You do have to be honest with the situation. When times are difficult state facts as you know them. Reassure people by saying "I don't know right now, but we will figure this out."

My second observation is **GOD promises to deliver HIS people from oppression.** GOD created humans with free will to choose HIM. Because Satan tricked humans to sin, we all have a part of us that does not want to choose GOD. This is known as our sin nature. There are people who will spend their entire lives listening to the sin nature while rejecting GOD's voice. They may cause harm on you and me. GOD allows us to have free will and knows that people will try to harm us. HE does not interfere the way we think HE should. But HE is in control and does hear our cry when we go through pain and HE promises deliverance.

My last observation is **GOD owns the better place**. We dream of what it looks like to be successful, but GOD has a place that is far beyond our dreams. HE told Moses that HE would take HIS people into the "*land of milk and honey.*" HIS description of the land provides a delicious flavor, appealing to their sense of taste and self-preservation. GOD not only wants to deliver us, but provide for us in ways beyond our understanding. I am not a prosperity teacher. But I do believe that GOD does not mean for you to go through this much pain without reward. **GOD provides and rewards**.

GOD Does Something About Your Problems

Trust can be a difficult concept to wrap our arms around when things are not going as planned, but is necessary for our growth. We have to trust that GOD sees those who place obstacles in our path and abhors it. Why do you think GOD revealed what HE performed through Moses?

I believe GOD wants you to learn leadership lessons from Bible leaders who went through difficult times. Read Exodus chapters 5– 11, 16, 19, 20, 25 and 37 to gain deeper insights to the observations I will make about great leadership and sometimes poor leadership; to make adjustments in your **Persuasive Ark,** and to lead your team.

Exodus 5:1 – 2 –

Afterward Moses and Aaron went in and told Pharaoh, "Thus says the Lord God of Israel: 'Let My people go, that they may hold a feast to Me in the wilderness.' "

2 And Pharaoh said, "Who is the Lord, that I should obey His voice to let Israel go? I do not know the Lord, nor will I let Israel go."

Moses and Aaron trusted GOD and delivered the difficult message. You would think that GOD would have simply wiped-out Pharaoh for not being obedient. But GOD was doing something greater. HE was about to wipe out the entire Egyptian culture of tyranny. Have you underestimated what GOD is really doing in your life? **This is the first warning GOD gave to Pharaoh to let HIS people go**. Are you prepared to deliver difficult messages?

GOD promised HE would perform signs that would cause the Egyptians to let HIS people go. HE performed ten plagues on Egypt, causing them to leave. During this time Aaron's rod became a serpent. I will explain the significance of this later.

Exodus 7:10 – 12 –

10 *So Moses and Aaron went in to Pharaoh, and they did so,*
just as the Lord commanded. And Aaron cast down his rod before
Pharaoh and before his servants, and it became a serpent.

11 *But Pharaoh also called the wise men and the sorcerers; so*
the magicians of Egypt, they also did in like manner with
their enchantments. 12 *For every man threw down his rod, and they*
became serpents. But Aaron's rod swallowed up their rods.

GOD's power is more powerful than magic. The example given to us shows a supernatural layer that humans can tap into that is evil, but hardly an opposition to GOD. HIS love is pure and so is HIS power. HE demonstrated HIS power to Pharaoh, but his heart was hardened. Did you see what Aaron's rod did? Pharaoh's magicians were able to do a couple of things GOD did, but they soon found out that HIS power is far greater than theirs.

As a leader, **seeing GOD as all-powerful, versus magical is important**. It sets our expectations of HIS deliverance. Our relationship is based on how we view HIM. GOD, the all-powerful, chooses to wait on us to invite HIM in our lives. HE wants more than a grocery list of things HE can grant. HE wants a loving, two-way relationship.

GOD's power is persistent. The harder Pharaoh's heart became, the more GOD pressed on him. HE performed ten plagues that had significance. GOD owns vengeance and does it HIS way.

I will challenge you to reflect on your leadership style as you read what happened during and after each plague. See yourself as the person being delivered, or the person helping to deliver people in these examples. Okay, you may have to see yourself as Pharaoh if there are some stubborn tendencies that you recognize.

Surrender to GOD

Plague 1 – Water Becomes Blood – The Need for a Savior, Shepherd and Sustainer.

Exodus 7:19 –

19 Then the Lord spoke to Moses, "Say to Aaron, 'Take your rod and stretch out your hand over the waters of Egypt, over their streams, over their rivers, over their ponds, and over all their pools of water, that they may become blood. And there shall be blood throughout all the land of Egypt, both in buckets of wood and pitchers of stone.' "

Did you see what GOD said to Moses? "Say to Aaron." More than likely GOD turned the water into blood, representing the murdered children thrown into the river. Egyptian magicians were able to turn water into blood as well. This made Pharaoh's heart hard because he saw that his people could do a trick. GOD was preparing the deliverance of HIS people. Moses and Aaron took the first step even though they were afraid.

Have you ever been afraid? Being afraid is not a problem. **It's when you are afraid and cannot move, that it becomes a problem**. GOD helps you take the step that takes you out of the problem when you are afraid. What is your first step to getting out of your current situation? How will you trust GOD? What message of encouragement do you need to tell your team right now? *Write your answers in your **Persuasive Ark.***

GOD touched the very thing that would sustain life by turning it into blood. For seven days, the river ran with blood and any stored water had to be poured out. They could not escape the blood.

We cannot escape the blood of JESUS either. HE became a human to save our eternal lives, but also to save our earthly lives, making them abundant. We need GOD as our Savior, Shepherd and Sustainer to save us, guide us daily and to provide for us.

GOD Is First

Plague 2 – Frogs – The Need to Get Rid of Idols.

Exodus 8:5 –

5 Then the Lord spoke to Moses, "Say to Aaron, 'Stretch out your hand with your rod over the streams, over the rivers, and over the ponds, and cause frogs to come up on the land of Egypt.' "

Wait! There it is again. "Say to Aaron." Egyptians worshiped frogs as a god or an idol. The true GOD showed humor here by making a ridiculous number of frogs appear that could not help the Egyptians.

Pharaoh begged Moses to have the frogs stop. GOD caused the frogs to die and there was a stench that made people sick. But Pharaoh hardened his heart once the people were able to clean up the dead frogs. GOD continued to prepare for the deliverance.

Are you revering a certain human as a person who can save your business? Some singers can be idols, but also business people, who have perceived success can be looked upon in reverence.

Are you believing that GOD can work through you to raise people up as leaders and to be cleansed by the blood of JESUS? "Cleansed by the blood" is a term meaning believe in CHRIST for salvation and for daily guidance. Ponder how you will help people self-discover CHRIST.

*Write this in your **Persuasive Ark**.*

GOD's Children Need Love and Respect

Plague 3 – Lice – The Need to Treat All Humans with Respect

Exodus 8:16 –

[16] So the Lord said to Moses, "Say to Aaron, 'Stretch out your rod, and strike the dust of the land, so that it may become lice throughout all the land of Egypt.' "

That's the third time. "Say to Aaron." GOD spoke to Moses and Moses spoke to Aaron. GOD does the same for you. HE speaks to you about your business or job and you will instruct the people out of the trouble and pain. I also notice Aaron's rod again. Lice were impure to the Egyptians. They also treated the Hebrews as impure. This is the third time Aaron used his rod. GOD did not tell Moses to tell Pharaoh to let HIS people go this time. HE just performed the plague. One step closer to GOD's deliverance.

How do you view other cultures and the opposite gender? Is anyone lower to you? How about above you? GOD made you the leader. **You can be a servant leader who is in charge, yet serves those who work for you**. You have an opportunity to see beyond differences and grow each person you encounter to perform better. Understand that people get scared too. Calm people down when you are scared.

Pause and take time to speak to GOD when things are difficult. Ask HIM what words you can use to tell people what is going on while bringing them peace. Your family, friends, workers and customers are your flock. They may not be ready or able to hear every detail about the difficult situation. In fact, many people may not be able to handle the situation at all. Use discernment when discussing difficulties to your flock.

*Write how you will bring peace to your flock in your **Persuasive Ark**.*

Plague 4 – Flies – The Need to Deal with Stubbornness

Exodus 8:20 – 21 –

20 And the Lord said to Moses, "Rise early in the morning and stand before Pharaoh as he comes out to the water. Then say to him, 'Thus says the Lord: "Let My people go, that they may serve Me. 21 Or else, if you will not let My people go, behold, I will send swarms of flies on you and your servants, on your people and into your houses. The houses of the Egyptians shall be full of swarms of flies, and also the ground on which they stand.

GOD turns from speaking to Aaron through Moses to speaking to Pharaoh through Moses. **This is also the fourth warning HE gave to Pharaoh to let HIS people go**. GOD sent flies which were not worshiped, but revered as persistent. I believe the flies represent the Egyptians' stubbornness. Their homes the slaves built would no longer be comfortable.

Where are you in terms of listening to GOD? HIS deliverance seemed like it was going slowly for the children of Israel, but it was definitely happening. Have you ever faced; or are you facing a very persistent, stubborn problem that comes back over and over? GOD's deliverance for you is on the way. Is there something you are fighting GOD over that you may need to surrender?

*Write this in your **Persuasive Ark.***

GOD Separates HIS Own for Protection

Plague 5 – Diseased Livestock – The Need to Join GOD's Plan

Exodus 9:1 – 5 –

Then the Lord said to Moses, "Go in to Pharaoh and tell him, 'Thus says the Lord God of the Hebrews: "Let My people go, that they may serve Me.
2 For if you refuse to let them go, and still hold them,
3 behold, the hand of the Lord will be on your cattle in the field, on the horses, on the donkeys, on the camels, on the oxen, and on the sheep—a very severe pestilence.
4 And the Lord will make a difference between the livestock of Israel and the livestock of Egypt. So nothing shall die of all that belongs to the children of Israel." '
" 5 Then the Lord appointed a set time, saying, "Tomorrow the Lord will do this thing in the land."

This is the fifth time GOD told Pharaoh to let HIS people go. This time HE mentions "Hebrews," which were looked down on by the Egyptians. Shepherds and herdsmen were viewed as the worst. Generations prior to Moses, Joseph told his brothers to tell the Pharaoh of that time that they were herdsmen. Eventually they were placed over all of the Egyptians' cattle and all animals.

Here, GOD is demonstrating that HE is making a distinction between the Israelites and the Egyptians. **GOD let Pharaoh believe he was in control when he really wasn't**. GOD killed all the Egyptian cattle and left the Israelite cattle healthy.

I believe the way GOD helps with the hardening of someone's heart is to allow them to believe they are in control and that they do not need HIM. How do you view people who work for you? Half of the plagues are done. GOD is still working on HIS deliverance. Are you relying on your own abilities too much? Are you relying on someone else to make you wealthy without you growing people? What is GOD's plan for you and are you participating in HIS plan?

Write this in your ***Persuasive Ark***.

Plague 6 – Boils – The Need to Make the Hidden Known

Exodus 9:8 – 12 –

[8] So the Lord said to Moses and Aaron, "Take for yourselves handfuls of ashes from a furnace, and let Moses scatter it toward the heavens in the sight of Pharaoh. [9] And it will become fine dust in all the land of Egypt, and it will cause boils that break out in sores on man and beast throughout all the land of Egypt

Unfortunately for the Egyptians, GOD stopped talking for a moment. This plague happened without an opportunity to stop it from coming. Pharaoh may have thought that he was getting away with harming people and lying about letting the people go. But GOD saw through his lies. There was nothing hidden from GOD.

Extreme grace taken for granted seems to also contribute to a hard heart. I am not talking about a sin that you cannot seem to stop doing; but rather, a rebellious heart that does not believe in the need for GOD to do anything for humans or that there is a need for HIS deliverance.

The hard-hearted person may even attack GOD, thinking HE will not respond. We see here that HE does respond to those who openly oppose HIM.

I believe this is the first miracle of multiplication. GOD took a small number of ashes and turned them into a dust storm that entered houses, locked rooms and boxes with lids. All Egyptian mammals would contract boils because of Pharaoh's hard heartedness. Anyone could see who was affected by GOD and who wasn't.

There was no hiding from GOD. Is there a hidden belief that you have that may oppose GOD? *Write this in your* ***Persuasive Ark***. GOD's deliverance was coming. All the Israelites had to do was hold on. Same for you. **Hold on. HE will deliver you**.

GOD Needs Your Faithfulness

Plague 7 – Hail – The Need for Unwavering Conviction for GOD

Exodus 9:18 – 19 –

[18] *Behold, tomorrow about this time I will cause very heavy hail to rain down, such as has not been in Egypt since its founding until now.* [19] *Therefore send now and gather your livestock and all that you have in the field, for the hail shall come down on every man and every animal which is found in the field and is not brought home; and they shall die." ' "*

This is the seventh plague and the sixth time GOD told Pharaoh to let HIS people go. The thought of this plague scared some of Pharaoh's servants to the point of putting cattle and servants in their homes. Moses held his rod out this time and GOD sent thunder, hail and fire down, destroying precious crops and killing livestock of those who did not heed the warning.

At first Pharaoh looked like he would repent, but once the trouble was gone, he and his servants hardened their hearts. Do you promise to "never do it again" when trouble is near and take back your promise when times are good? **Your leadership is more effective when you are consistent.**

Moses's leadership was becoming more and more prevalent. He was able to hold up his hand and the hail stopped. This plague is very similar to the plague that is predicted in the book of Revelation. I suggest you take a look at Revelation chapter 16 to compare. GOD is making you a leader. HIS deliverance is almost here. Is there a part of your leadership that could be more consistent? Do you believe GOD is working on HIS deliverance through you?

Write this in your ***Persuasive Ark.***

Plague 8 – Locusts – The Need to Address Unhealthy Pride

Exodus 10:12 –

12 *Then the Lord said to Moses, "Stretch out your hand over the land of Egypt for the locusts, that they may come upon the land of Egypt, and eat every herb of the land—all that the hail has left."*

This is eighth plague and the seventh time GOD told Pharaoh to let HIS people go. As if large burning hail was not bad enough, GOD sent Moses and Aaron to tell Pharaoh that locusts would eat whatever food was left for the Egyptians.

Pharaoh's servants talked to him and said the city was destroyed; let the people go. Pharaoh said he would let the people go, but asked, "*Who are the ones that are going?*" When Moses said, "Everyone," Pharaoh tried to make up his own terms by saying the "men" could go for a little while. GOD told Moses to stretch his hand and locusts appeared that covered everything. I believe the locusts represent total destruction of wealth and sustainability due to pride.

Pharoah did not have a name in the Bible. To me, he represents a poor relationship with GOD. Pharaoh pridefully thought he was in control; he was stubborn when it came to listening to GOD's voice, was very demanding, and was proud of his title. He would not listen to warnings and fear drove his every decision and lie. After seven times, GOD would no longer warn Pharaoh to let HIS people go.

Fear of embarrassment can cause pride. Trying to keep up the appearance that you are in control or that you have it all together can one day be confronted with the truth that you may have neither. What fear do you have that is driving your decisions? Are you afraid to admit to people that things are not going as well as you expected? What is GOD asking you to do that you are refusing to do? **Let GOD deliver you from you.**

*Write this in your **Persuasive Ark.***

Plague 9 – Darkness – The Need to Drop Limiting Beliefs

Exodus 10:21 –

[21] *Then the Lord said to Moses, "Stretch out your hand toward heaven, that there may be darkness over the land of Egypt, darkness which may even be felt."*

GOD told Moses to stretch out his hand, then HE caused it to be supernaturally dark. The Egyptians worshiped the sun and gave it a name, the sun god Ra. For three days no Egyptian could see anything. It was like being in a deep cave with no lights, but something was constantly touching you. If you held your hand up, you would not be able to see it. The Egyptians could hear each other, but could not see anything.

I believe GOD was showing HIS relationship with those who believe in HIM versus those who don't. Moses did not know what was going to happen when GOD told him to raise his hand. GOD showed that by the raising of a hand of a believer, HE would do the vengeance or the miracle.

Darkness seems to be a demonstration of spiritual blindness, evil, lack of clarity or **limiting beliefs of superiority**. Ingenuity like fire, torches and candles would not work. GOD let the Egyptians remain in total darkness for three days. Does the number of days sound familiar? Three days is the number that JESUS stayed in the grave before being resurrected.

The children of Israel had full light in their houses. Pharaoh told Moses that the children of Israel could go. Moses said that Pharaoh must also give what little livestock was alive to the children of Israel to use as their sacrifices. Pharaoh told Moses that if he ever came back, he would be killed. This was Pharaoh's last chance to voluntarily let the people go.

What lessons in your life have you repeated? Do you need to surrender a mindset that you may have that blocks a great relationship with GOD?

*Write this in your **Persuasive Ark.***

Staying in GOD's Limits

Plague 10 – Death of the Firstborn – The Need to Know There is a Limit to Life

Exodus 11:4 – 6 –

4 Then Moses said, "Thus says the Lord: 'About midnight I will
go out into the midst of Egypt; 5 and all the firstborn in the land of
Egypt shall die, from the firstborn of Pharaoh who sits on his
throne, even to the firstborn of the female servant who is behind the
handmill, and all the firstborn of the animals. 6 Then there shall be
a great cry throughout all the land of Egypt, such as was not like
it before, nor shall be like it again.

After seven warnings to let HIS people go and nine plagues, GOD allowed the tenth plague to happen, causing the Egyptians to give up the fight. They had finally crossed the line of no return.

The plagues end where the **Personal Ark** began. One Pharaoh told the Hebrew women to throw their children into the river and kill them. Pharaoh had no regard for life and sentenced the Hebrews to a life of cruelty.

There was no way to persuade a Pharaoh who was full of pride. GOD struck down every firstborn, male and female, human or animal. GOD gave a condition that would save a household from experiencing death. The household had to put the blood of a lamb over the door so the angel would *pass over* the household.

JESUS died during the Passover week. HE died for the sins of mankind. Just like the Israelites who believed enough to put blood over their door, we must believe in the blood of the LAMB. JESUS's blood was shed to save you and me. HE stayed in the grave three days, but on Sunday morning, HE arose! Hallelujah!

Does your **Persuasive Ark** contain a relationship with JESUS? Do you think the people around you need to hear about JESUS from someone else? Will you share your testimony about your relationship with JESUS to other people? Are you putting off allowing GOD to lead your life while you seek wealth and fame?

After the death of the firstborn, Pharaoh did in fact let the people go. The women of Israel did as GOD said. They asked the Egyptian households for their gold and silver. The Egyptians did not need it. Dead bodies of humans and animals were all over the place. Buildings and temples were burned and broken.

The Egyptians gladly gave away their gold. Perhaps some of them were saying, "I'm sorry." Perhaps some of them were scared that something else would happen. Whatever the case, the children of Israel were finally free!

Receiving Complaints

But **one month into the trip**, the people complained about leaving Egypt. They just saw ten horrible plagues fall on the Egyptians, yet they complained about the lack of comforts.

Exodus 16:1 – 3 –

And they journeyed from Elim, and all the congregation of the children of Israel came to the Wilderness of Sin, which is between Elim and Sinai, on the fifteenth day of the second month after they departed from the land of Egypt. 2 Then the whole congregation of the children of Israel complained against Moses and Aaron in the wilderness. 3 And the children of Israel said to them, "Oh, that we had died by the hand of the Lord in the land of Egypt, when we sat by the pots of meat and when we ate bread to the full! For you have brought us out into this wilderness to kill this whole assembly with hunger."

Complaints came up quickly. The children of Israel were excited to leave Egypt, but when it got a little hard, they said something about it. Does this sound familiar with your business or job? People who have not bought into the purpose of your business will question your direction and leadership style.

Complaints make you susceptible to decisions that will make you hurry or worry. This is where the **Persuasive Ark** is needed most. Things will not go as planned. You have to remember what GOD brought you through in the past and believe HE will continue to deliver you.

Responding to Complaints

Exodus 16:9 –

9 *Then Moses spoke to Aaron, "Say to all the congregation of the children of Israel, 'Come near before the Lord, for He has heard your complaints.' "*

Requests are one thing, complaints are another. The children of Israel did not like GOD's plan and began to complain about HIS servants, Moses and Aaron. As a leader, especially if you are appointed by GOD, you can expect those who follow you to complain.

Let's be honest, complaints hurt. I believe GOD feels the complaint in ways we cannot understand. We may be telling HIM HE is not enough. You can also expect complaints to come from your customers. How will you respond? GOD is patient and gentle.

Slow the Process (STP) – **Slow down and respond well**. Use *Reactive Forgiveness* from *Active Forgiveness: Freedom to Be a Leader*.

GOD Provides and Wants to Be GOD

Manna was collected.

Exodos 16:11 – 16 –

[11] And the Lord spoke to Moses, saying, [12] "I have heard the complaints of the children of Israel. Speak to them, saying, 'At twilight you shall eat meat, and in the morning you shall be filled with bread. And you shall know that I am the Lord your God.' "

[13] So it was that quail came up at evening and covered the camp, and in the morning the dew lay all around the camp. [14] And when the layer of dew lifted, there, on the surface of the wilderness, was a small round substance, as fine as frost on the ground. [15] So when the children of Israel saw it, they said to one another, "What is it?" For they did not know what it was.

And Moses said to them, "This is the bread which the Lord has given you to eat. [16] This is the thing which the Lord has commanded: 'Let every man gather it according to each one's need, one omer for each person, according to the number of persons; let every man take for those who are in his tent.' "

I read this passage and thought it was about GOD being a provider. It is. But I also see GOD's heart. "*And you shall know that I am the Lord your God.*" HE fought with Pharaoh and the Egyptians, telling them that HE is GOD. Now HE is fighting with the people HE delivered out of bondage to tell them the same thing.

GOD wants to be GOD in your life. HE provides purpose, cares, protects, sees you as special and is all-powerful. HE made you special and loves you deeply. I do not believe GOD responded to their complaints, rather that HE wanted the children of Israel to succeed. HE provided food that was not from this world. They had to collect it each day, otherwise it would rot.

Is GOD, <u>GOD</u> in your life? Have you reduced HIM to a simple wishing well who punishes you if you are not perfect? GOD feels your pain. HE can orchestrate a situation that seems difficult at the time, but is there to grow you as HIS leader. HE does not need you to be JESUS, but to become like HIM more and more each day. Will you let GOD be GOD versus trying to make HIM a wishing well?

In Exodus 19 and 20, GOD had Moses meet HIM on top of Mount Sinai and gave HIM **the Ten Commandments written on stone tablets**. Moses got angry at the people when they made a golden calf as an idol because he was gone forty days. GOD made another set of tablets. These were to be placed in the Ark of the Covenant.

GOD Wants HIS Protection Remembered

The contents of the Ark of the Covenant are the Jar of Manna, the Ten Commandments and Aaron's Rod.

GOD told Moses to make an ark.

Exodus 25:10 –

10 "And they shall make an ark of acacia wood;

GOD needed a place to place the Ten Commandments into.

From the garden of Eden to today, GOD loves when we mimic HIS love. But HE also sees those who oppose what HE stands for. I pondered the Ten Commandment and at one time thought they were a list of rules created to take "fun" out of life. But when I reread Exodus 20, **I see that GOD wants to give us protection**.

As I stated earlier, GOD seems to enjoy being invited into our lives and plans. I believe HE gave us clarity on how to keep HIS protection when HE gave us the Ten Commandments and other parts of the Law.

Let's look at the first two commandments to see HIS protection.

Exodus 20:1 – 6 –

And God spoke all these words, saying:

2 *"I am the Lord your God, who brought you out of the land of Egypt, out of the house of bondage.*

3 *"You shall have no other gods before Me.*

4 *"You shall not make for yourself a carved image—any likeness of anything that is in heaven above, or that is in the earth beneath, or that is in the water under the earth;* 5 *you shall not bow down to them nor serve them. For I, the Lord your God, am a jealous God, visiting the iniquity of the fathers upon the children to*

the third and fourth generations of those who hate Me, [6] but showing mercy to thousands, to those who love Me and keep My commandments.

When I see the commandments, I think of GOD telling me not to place my trust in a god that cannot save me. I can also hear HIM gently saying that making an idol out of anything above, on or under the earth would cause me to misplace my trust.

HE is telling you that you can trust HIM and HIS power. HE is also telling you to make an effort to remember the way HE protects you. HE made a special place for the commandments which is the Ark of the Covenant and wants us to do the same. Your **Persuasive Ark** is a special place to write things, but your heart is where you keep them. There is only one commandment that you need to be concerned about these days, namely, **love one another**. Place that in your heart.

Exodus 25:16 –

[16] And you shall put into the ark the Testimony which I will give you.

Exodus 37:1 –

Then Bezalel made the ark of acacia wood;

Remember your **Personal Ark**? Care and protection of your skilled community helps you influence them to get the work completed. GOD gave Bezalel skills to make and decorate the ark. He did this with the gifts and talents GOD gave him. He also was told to use his skills by Moses.

Will you see that GOD is trying to protect you from the enemy and sometimes from yourself? Will you remember the commandments that GOD has given and have the mindset that HE is trying to care for you and protect you?

Let's look at how GOD has provided for you.

GOD Wants HIS Provision Remembered

Manna kept in a jar.

Exodus 16:33 – 36 –

33 *And Moses said to Aaron, "Take a pot and put an omer of manna in it, and lay it up before the Lord, to be kept for your generations."* 34 *As the Lord commanded Moses, so Aaron laid it up before the Testimony, to be kept.* 35 *And the children of Israel ate manna forty years, until they came to an inhabited land; they ate manna until they came to the border of the land of Canaan.* 36 *Now an omer is one-tenth of an ephah.*

GOD told Moses to tell Aaron to save a jar of manna. This was not because they did not have a refrigerator or plastic wrap. GOD wanted to show the children of Israel how HE provided for them during their entire time in the wilderness and all of their lives.

Each day the Israelites were supposed to scoop up enough of the supernatural bread from heaven to feed their family. If they tried to save any for another day, it would rot and stink. GOD wanted total reliance on HIM being the provider.

But this sample of manna never rotted. I can imagine Aaron and Moses holding up the jar every now and then to keep everyone encouraged that GOD was still providing.

No human could take credit for the strange food. It could not be reverse engineered or copycatted. They were in the wilderness with no way to do farming.

GOD provides for you, but maybe not in the way you would like. Many of the Israelites may have gotten tired of the same food, every day for forty years. But they were provided for. They were on the brink of a land where they could enjoy a variety and where life was easy. The grapes were so large that it took two men to carry it!

How has GOD provided for you? *Write this down in your* ***Persuasive Ark*** *to keep yourself encouraged.* We have seen GOD's protection and HIS provision, now let's see HIS power.

GOD Wants HIS Power Remembered

Aaron's staff was used in many miracles.

Numbers 17:8 –

[8] Now it came to pass on the next day that Moses went into the tabernacle of witness, and behold, the rod of Aaron, of the house of Levi, had sprouted and put forth buds, had produced blossoms and yielded ripe almonds.

Numbers 8:10 – 11 –

[10] And the Lord said to Moses, "Bring Aaron's rod back before the Testimony, to be kept as a sign against the rebels, that you may put their complaints away from Me, lest they die." [11] Thus did Moses; just as the Lord had commanded him, so he did.

I remember being so sick that it felt like there was no end to the pain. I was thinking about going out, so I may have worked out a little harder to be ready for the club. I had chest pains that seemed to suddenly hit me. The pain was so intense that I did not trust myself to drive. I could barely breathe. Of course I prayed. Isn't that what you are supposed to do when trouble hits?

I immediately thought of sins I did for years, trying to rationalize the pain and beg for forgiveness. During the prayer, I felt a small amount of relief. Minutes later, the pain subsided to the point that I could breathe. I called a neighbor who took me to the doctor. He said he could not find anything seriously wrong, but that I had a bruised sternum from lifting weights and an acute amount of gas. He could not prescribe anything, but told me to take over the counter medication.

GOD got my attention. I was hurt, scared and alone. After this encounter, I said I would remember this story of how GOD healed my body. When times were difficult, I remembered this story for a while, until I went through other difficulties to replace this story.

Unfortunately, any promises I made to GOD during the prayer slowly faded from my mind.

What has GOD taken you through? Has the memory of HIS deliverance faded? What promise did HE make to you and kept over the years? Your **Persuasive Ark** is there for you to remember what GOD has brought you through so you can use the story to encourage yourself. When you are tempted to give up or give into something you should not, use the deliverance stories as a place you can go to regain confidence in GOD.

GOD's power is special and something we easily forget when times are going well. We quickly forget there is a supernatural element to life when trouble comes. We try to jump in with our own plans instead of asking GOD what plan we should follow.

Does this sound familiar in your life? Are you willing to ask GOD, "What do YOU want me to do?" when times get hard? This requires looking for answers in the Bible.

Your **Persuasive Ark** should now contain how you will lead and influence each team member to get the work done. It should also contain your conviction to keep going when you face trials. Lastly, it should contain how you will add trust in the LORD as your new skill, especially when life rushes at you all at once.

WARNING

- Admit when you are scared, overwhelmed and when things are not going as planned.
- Avoid trying to keep up appearances that things are going well with your business, but figure out how to bring peace to your team when things are going wrong.
- Avoid walking alone for too long.

NEXT STEPS

- Add a prayer partner to your team who you can confide in.
- Add monthly dates to your calendar where you will revisit the **Persuasive Ark** and update it.
- Be prepared for difficult situations by knowing yourself and addressing any trust issues you may have with GOD.

How does it work?

Putting It All Together

When I realized that GOD made me for HIS purpose, I started seeing people and situations differently. I saw that I needed people more than I thought. I was excited that I could do a lot by myself, but when I realized that I could get more accomplished with people, I had to ask GOD to put the right crowd around me.

By now, you may have decided to add at least one person to your team, namely a prayer partner. If you do not have the resources for additional people ,then GOD will grant you the wisdom for the skills you need. But whether you work alone or have a team, you should define the purpose of your product or service, know and define how you will make adjustments to work with internal or external teams, and define how you will remain resilient during difficult times.

Changing the Mindset

Why did I use arks for you to build? It was a discovery I made during my quiet time I spend with the LORD daily. I found out there were only three arks built in the Bible. I asked GOD the significance and HE guided me to make the connection of purpose, personal growth and persuasion to HIS message of love for you. HE wants to grow you as you grow your business.

> Leadership Tip #6 – You were made wonderfully and carefully by GOD to be HIS leader.

Working with People Who Think Different Than Me

Each ark you build will need prayer. GOD will guide you to understand your needs enough to ask HIM. The prayer is not to inform HIM, but to invite HIM and to surrender to HIM.

Purpose Ark – By now you have written down the purpose of your product or service and have written out specific instructions for each role you will play, outsource or hire for.

Personal Ark – By now you have written down who you are as a person. You should also have a plan to address moods and how your style can be adjusted to work with a variety of people. You should have also included how you will work with a prayer partner.

Persuasive Ark – By now you have written down specific expectations and deliverables for each role and developed an RFP and possibly an SOW. You should also have how you will address difficult times and how GOD has brought you through situations.

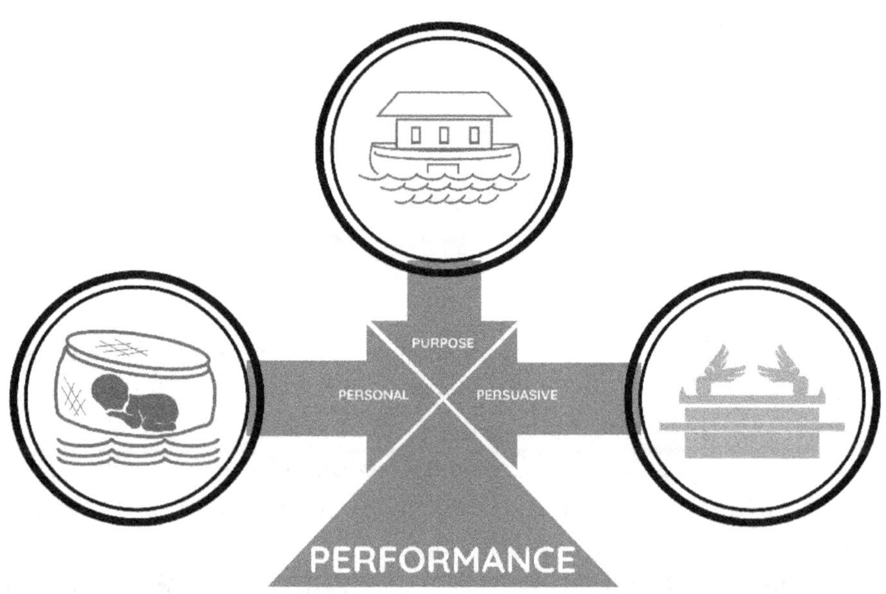

Performance, otherwise known as productivity, is the goal of building a skilled community. The work needs to get done and you are the leader who will guide people to their peak performance. You will also have patience enough to guide people who are underperforming to a place of performance.

Write out your purpose for each role. Make personal adjustments to work with people. And use your influence to persuade people to perform at optimal levels.

There may be a few who you may not be able to work with. But if you find yourself with a lot of people leaving your company, then consider revisiting the **Personal Ark** to make adjustments on your style.

Working with other people is important because GOD placed you in business to interact with people.

Be the Expert

Knowing yourself is important. You have just read how to define the necessary skills it will take to minimally run your business. Will you take these steps? My challenge to you is to be different by allowing GOD to grow you in areas that you are not familiar with.

Fear should no longer hold you back! You can do this! GOD made you the expert. Repeat these words, "I am the expert!" Now be it!

Prayers to Guide Your Purpose

Dear LORD, please guide my purpose to be used more and more by YOU. Please open my eyes to the people YOU provide and help me guide their purpose to perform to reach the destination YOU set before us. amen.

Dear LORD, please grow me. Help me to appreciate how YOU made me. Help me to understand other people so I can work well with them. Help me to bring out the best in people. amen.

Dear LORD, please help me care, protect and see value in others so I can influence them to their highest performance. Help me to serve those who are working with me. Bless our efforts. amen.

In JESUS NAME, Amen.

Leadership Tip #7 – Leaders recognize prayer is the most important conversation they can ever have.

WARNING

- Underestimating your calling to be a leader could have you making decisions that are safe and that you can control when decisions that require trust are needed.
- Overestimating your abilities as a leader you learned from the world's leadership may cause you to overlook or devalue the teachings of CHRIST as your leader.

NEXT STEPS

- Ask GOD to help you trust in HIS plan.
- Ask yourself: "Why am I not trusting GOD to handle this situation?"
- Schedule time on your calendar to think about the things that worry you. Limit this to a single day or hour.
- Place your worries in front of GOD, and for each worry, give HIM praise.

About the Author

Stan Washington is a teacher of the Bible, not a preacher. He accepted the LORD at the age of 12. He walked away from serving GOD in college and pursued fulfilling his own desires. His pursuit led him to barely finish college. He became a programmer but wanted to get into learning about the business world. Still empty, he returned to the LORD wanting to get his life in order. He took many continuing education classes at a Bible Institute.

Later, he joined the largest quick service restaurant and became a McDonald's executive over Operations and Technology. After many years he turned to entrepreneurism and became the founder and president of Honor Services Office, a software company that helps small businesses grow in CHRIST as they grow their business. He is ready to share the tips he learned from his experiences while enabling a community of prayer to truly follow JESUS. Stan is the author of GOD-Centered Business: A Foundational Framework to Grow with Resilience, Active Forgiveness: Freedom to Be a Leader and also is the co-author of Plans to Prosper: Strategies, Systems and Tools for Small Business Marketing Success.

He is married and has two children. He has traveled to Zimbabwe, China, Mexico, and many places in the United States to spread the great news about JESUS.

Contact:

Facebook: @HonorServicesOffice and GOD-Centered Business: Global People of All Colors

LinkedIn: Honor Services God Centered Business

Instagram : **@HonorServicesOffice**

https://www.HonorServicesOffice.com

YouTube: https://www.youtube.com/@honorservicesoffice

Author's Daily Devotional *(This is my quiet time)*
https://www.facebook.com/groups/honordevotional

https://honordevotional.blogspot.com

Other Do it Yourself Resources

Here are some other resources you can leverage to help grow your business:

Business Foundation

This study guide includes visioning, resilience testing, marketing, sales and customer service tips and a 36-day devotional.

***GOD-Centered Business: A Foundational Framework to Grow with Resilience Copyright 2021 ISBN:* 978-0-9909831-6-3**

Leadership Development

This study guide includes a different approach to stress management, regaining sleep while increasing lost sense of identity and trust.

***ACTIVE FORGIVENESS: Freedom to be a Leader Copyright 2026 ISBN:* 978-0-9909831-7-0**

GOD-Centered Business Presentation

There is also a presentation that goes with the class. The presentation is for use with the GOD-centered Business class and can be downloaded from www.honorservices office.com. Feel free to use this in print or presentation format.

Marketing Growth Tools

***Plans to Prosper: Strategies, Systems and Tools for Small Business Marketing Success (Victoria Cook and Stan Washington) Copyright 2015 ISBN:* 978-0-9909831-0-1**

Business Management Software

Honor Services Office is a small business management tool that provides an easy to use CRM, Online invoice / Bookkeeping System and Content Marketing system.

Visit **https://www.HonorServicesOffice.com**

www.ingramcontent.com/pod-product-compliance
Lightning Source LLC
LaVergne TN
LVHW010926110826
845149LV00013B/2498

* 9 7 8 0 9 9 0 9 8 3 1 8 7 *